Two Sides to Every Story

Ethics, Dilemmas and Points of View

Discussion, Writing, Improvisation

Written by Greta Barclay Lipson, Ed.D.

Illustrated by Judy Hierstein

A revised and expanded edition of the previously published
Tales with a Twist book by Good Apple.

Teaching & Learning Company

1204 Buchanan St., P.O. Box 10
Carthage, IL 62321-0010

This book belongs to

_____

Dedication

There were three empty spaces in the family, waiting to be filled, when fate played its poetic, random game and brought us Susan, Lorene and Jane.

Three young women—different, yet alike: intelligent, fair featured and spirited! We claim their elegance among three more expansive gifts bestowed on us. In honor of that twist of fate, we gratefully dedicate this book to them.

We love them, not for comely grace alone.

My enduring gratitude to Geraldine N. Barclay for editing the original manuscript.

Cover art by Judy Hierstein

Copyright © 2004, Teaching & Learning Company

ISBN No. 1-57310-439-6

Printing No. 987654321

Teaching & Learning Company
1204 Buchanan St., P.O. Box 10
Carthage, IL 62321-0010

Table of Contents

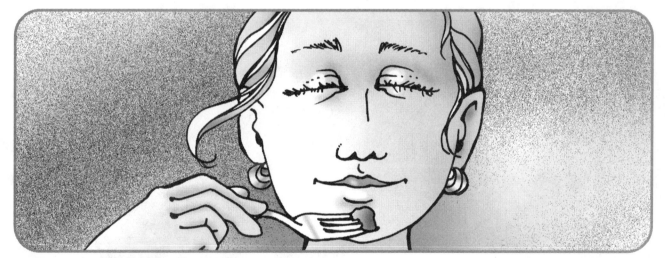

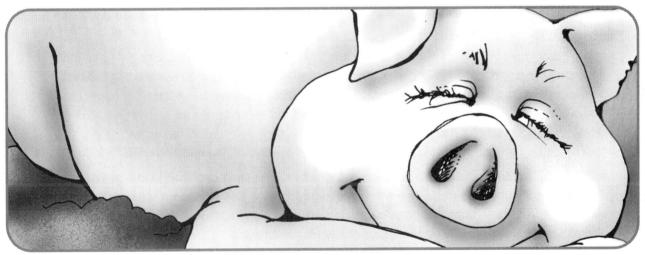

Dear Teacher or Parent,

These tales are explorations of mystery, danger, comedy and human nonsense from sources old and new. The stories in this book were deliberately chosen because they are dramatic incidents with strange and evocative endings. Each vignette lends itself to a search for answers to difficult questions. Every selection is the basis for a lesson plan and activities which include discussion, improvisation and writing.

Is a thief less a thief for stealing food? Is it true that what you don't know won't hurt you? Is there truly a sucker born every minute? Is your anatomy your destiny? Do we reap as we have sown? No single answer can resolve a dilemma or a conflict but therein lies the learning!

It would be foolish to deny the role of fate in the scenario of our lives or to deny the inexorable forces of nature or the unremitting effect of social class on all of us. There is so much that is in place for each of us at the time of birth that, some argue, we are almost programmed for our destiny. Others believe that we are the controllers of our destiny. Included in this calculation, of course, is the effect of the country in which we live—and our relative freedom, repression, education or personal drive.

The eternal conflict between fate and free will has been examined throughout human history and is found, most notably, in the great plays of the ancient Greeks. In modern times the uncertainty of fate is characterized in works such as Robert Frost's poem, "The Road Not Taken." This selection is a cogent piece because it suggests that we do have some choices, and we do make daily decisions which influence our lives. To the degree that we can shape our own fate, we must learn to ask questions, assess information, make decisions and set standards for ethical behavior.

In my secondary school, of olden times, I believed that my English teachers really taught us about life as reflected in books. It seemed that literature teachers dealt with realistic concerns, about which we were invited to express an opinion and were taken seriously. Literature was a medium of socialization which helped us understand something of what the world was all about, because—more than history or science or mathematics or "the facts" as we know them—literature captures the essence of human behavior.

Educators are conduits of the human experience with all that implies—and significant stories are the magical materials with which they forge an awareness of the real world outside of the classroom. The stories are the stuff of life, exceeding the limits of what any one of us could possibly encounter personally (or would want to).

When literature does its job, it shows all of us how people and events work in society. One hopes that a sharpened perspective and new insights will help us understand much more about ourselves and enable us to do much better in taking charge of our own lives.

Sincerely,

Greta

Greta Barclay Lipson, Ed.D.

How to Use This Book

Each of the 10 tales in this book is a dramatic incident which acts as a basic lesson plan for activities. The format is consistent and flexible:

- The Story
- Point of View—Discussion Questions
- Improvisation—Role Play Variations
- Writing Suggestions
- Student Comment

When stories are evocative, they invite analysis and speculation through discussion. Among the many implicit questions in the selections are the following: What is the real issue in this story? What motivates people to do what they do? Why are the events disturbing or funny? Is anybody or anything accountable for the circumstances? If the decision were left to you, how would you have done something differently than the characters? And indeed—what were the alternatives? We learn slowly that all choices have consequences, and we can only speculate about what the outcomes may be. And perhaps, just perhaps, it is possible to stand up to fate.

Here, as always, the teacher is the guide from, ". . . the intelligent progression from cocksure ignorance to thoughtful probability." as succinctly expressed in Ashley Montague's book, *The Ignorance of Certainty*.

Chapter 1
Lady in the Cave

Lady in the Cave*

Synopsis

Emmis is a very serious man who leaves his home and family to search for the meaning of truth. He travels over the far reaches of the land when, haggard and depleted, he finds the Lady in the Cave on a mountaintop. Her name is Verity, and she is eternally dedicated to truth. Aged and frail, by the hardships of life, Emmis stays on as her student to learn the mysteries of truth. After a year of study and revelation, he prepares to leave and gratefully asks Verity what he can do to repay her kindness. Her response fills Emmis with consternation!

*Retold by Greta B. Lipson, Ed.D. from *Favorite Folktales from Around the World*, edited by Jane Yolen (New York: Random House, 1986)

Lady in the Cave

The Truth Shall Set You Free

Retold by Greta B. Lipson

There once was man by the name of Emmis who was highly respected in his town. He was known to be a most honest and upstanding citizen who was trusted by all. He was, however, a very serious person and was always searching for the meaning of truth. A man such as Emmis was rarely heard to laugh, and he was not much fun to be with. As a matter of fact, he had become terribly boring in his zealous pursuit of the truth and was generally avoided by those who were more light of heart!

Emmis plodded along—never satisfied that the ultimate secrets of honesty had been revealed to him. The fact that others were not so consumed was of little interest to him. One day he went to his wife and said, "I really must satisfy my yearning to know about the meaning of truth and how it is acquired; I believe I must go in search of the answers before I become too old to travel—for I have no way of knowing how long my quest will take."

His wife Martha was a strong and patient woman. After listening carefully to what her husband expressed, she responded with understanding, "I know how you have felt about this for your entire life, and I know how important this matter is to you. Do what you have to do and I will love you all the same. We shall all look forward to your return no matter how long it takes you." Some say she must have been relieved to be rid of her husband with his constantly furrowed brow and persistent musing!

Emmis left his home carrying a small knapsack since he did not want the burden of many belongings. He traveled very long distances each day and left his home farther and farther behind. He crossed rivers and streams, lakes and oceans, always looking for the truth. He visited small towns and villages and big bustling cities that were larger and more filled with people than anyplace he had ever imagined. He walked through the silence of dense woods and majestic forests in his fruitless search—but nothing was revealed to him. His threadbare clothes hung on his tired frame announcing to anyone who saw him that he was an exhausted man searching for something that was forever elusive.

One strange day Emmis found himself, unaccountably, at the very top of a mountain. He was drawn to a cave at a dizzying height, and when he looked into the cool, compelling darkness he saw the form of an old, bent woman. He knew intuitively that he had arrived at the place he had sought for so long. "Are you the Lady Truth?" he asked softly.

"Yes, I am," she answered slowly.

"May I come in and speak with you awhile?" he hesitated.

"Anyone who travels such a hard route to find me is always welcome," she responded. "Come in, please."

It was then, when Emmis was in the cave, that he saw by the firelight how very old and frail she was. Her skin was like wrinkled leather pulled over the fine bones of her face. She had few teeth in her mouth and her hair hung in pathetic, wispy strands. Her eyes were dimmed with age but she had a spiritual aura that softened her image with a magic luminosity.

They spoke haltingly because the man was shy, until he was so overcome with her wisdom that he was moved to ask a favor of her. "There is so much to talk about, and you have so much to teach me—may I stay? Will you accept me as your student?"

"Of course," she responded, and he was soon at his ease in her presence when she said, "My name is Verity. Please call me by my name."

Emmis stayed with her in the cave, barely noticing the passage of time, because he had so much to learn. He was an eager student and each day he sat and listened and asked questions. Finally one remarkable year had passed. Satisfied that Verity had imparted to him all that he could absorb, he announced that it was time for him to take his leave.

Standing at the mouth of the cave, Emmis was filled with emotion. "I am eternally grateful to you for all you have taught me about truth. Is there something I can do for you—some way I can repay you?"

Without hesitation Verity responded. "Since you are kind enough to offer," she said, "there is a favor I would ask of you."

She looked into his eyes. He waited. "When they ask about me—tell them that I am young and beautiful."

Lady in the Cave

Point of View—Discussion Questions

1. Why would Verity, who had devoted a lifetime to the examination of the meaning of truth, ask her student, Emmis, to tell an outrageous lie about her age and appearance when he returned to civilization?

Possible Answer

Perhaps Verity was being honest with herself and realistic about the values of our society. We place a great premium upon outward physical beauty and put much less emphasis upon the internal qualities of people which are not so quickly discernable. Neither age, nor intelligence, nor wisdom rank as important in the popular culture as youth and beauty—however we may protest to the contrary.

2. Explain how Emmis could tell everyone that Verity was beautiful and be absolutely honest about it.

3. When in search of meaningful or profound answers, why do many stories take the reader to distant and exotic places such as mountaintop, caves, and other remote areas? Is there more purity to be found away from the clamor of civilization?

4. Is truth constant, unwavering and absolute, or does truth change in different contexts, eras or circumstances? (In ancient times, the sun was thought to revolve around the Earth. People were punished for contradicting that truth.)

Lady in the Cave

Improvisation—Role Play Variations

1. Play the story as it reads. Include questions and answers in the dialogue which could have taken place in the cave. Partnerships or groups may participate in the role play after some planning sessions.

2. Entrepreneurs and assorted business types hear about Verity and set up a carnival atmosphere for profit at the top of the mountain where the Lady in the Cave resides. They advertise that the truth can be bought. Concerned citizens come to protest the commercialization of the message. They do not believe that the truth is an article of merchandise which can be purchased like groceries or other commodities. They believe that such offers are misleading and offensive to honest people.

3. The local politicians denounce Verity at a political rally because they are not sure what she is all about and what damage she can do to their reputations or their plans for the future. They are afraid of a crusade against corruption in government and what could be reveled in the name of truth and honesty in civic affairs. Public officials will appear at a speaker's forum to defend their turf. Each one intends to attack "the truth" as a public menace.

Lady in the Cave

Writing Suggestions

1. Write two paragraphs. In the first paragraph explain some of the advantages of telling the truth all of the time. In the second explain the disadvantages. What could happen to a dedicated truth-teller in the course of a school day? Is there a time for a "little white lie"? What exactly does that mean? When is silence golden?

2. As part of a group effort, write an after-school special which deals with the theme of honesty in school, business, or public life. What are some of the significant problems with dishonesty in a school environment and how does it affect students as individuals?

3. Verity is described as frail and elderly as the Lady in the Cave. Are elderly people generally described in stereotypic ways? The term *ageist* describes a prejudicial attitude toward old people. Sharpen your sensitivity toward this view. Keep a TV log of commercials and other media advertising which use older people. How are older citizens portrayed? Are they vigorous, bright and productive citizens or are they infirm, foolish and peculiar? What conclusions do you draw from your findings? Can one generalize about this group of people? Does wisdom and honesty come with age? Explain.

4. "To me, old age is always fifteen years older than I am." This is a quote from the American financier and adviser to Presidents, Bernard M. Baruch, on his eighty-fifth birthday, August 1955. In your view, how old is old?

Name _____

Lady in the Cave

The Truth Shall Set You Free
Student Comment

Characters: Verity, the Lady in the Cave
              Emmis, the truth seeker
              Martha, his wife

In a paragraph express your feelings about an aspect of this story which you liked or disliked. How would you have changed it?

Alternative: Now that the story has been discussed, explain the proverb above from your point of view.

_____

_____

_____

_____

_____

_____

_____

_____

_____

_____

_____

_____

_____

Chapter 2

You Can Take It with You

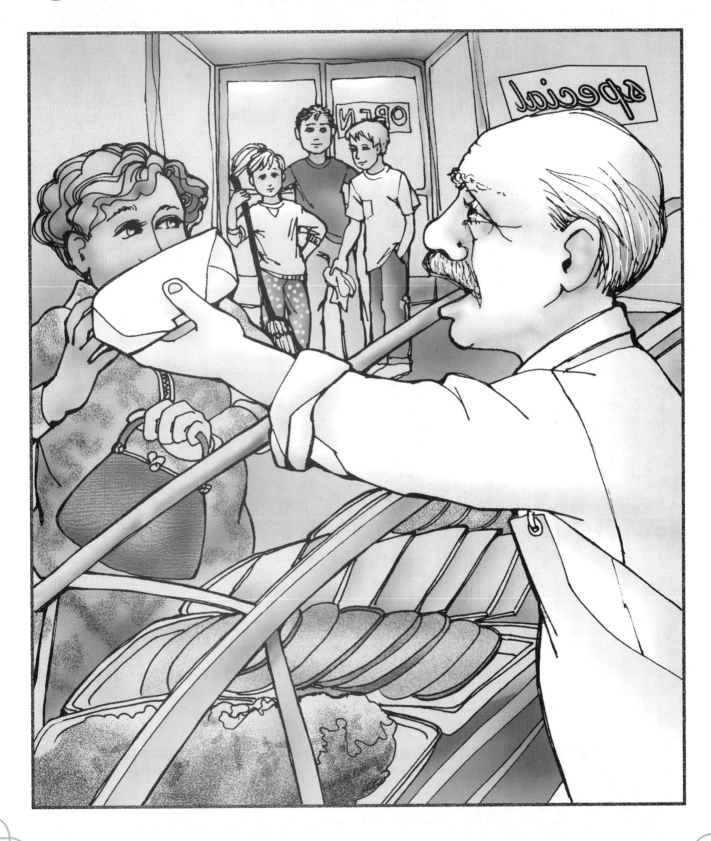

You Can Take It with You
Synopsis

Grampa Boris and his wife, Grandma Sophie, work very hard in the family delicatessen. They have three bright grandchildren living with them. The oldest grandson is Leon, the middle child is Daniel, and their little granddaughter is Becky. As young as they are, the children work hard in the store and are, for the most part, uncomplaining. They do, however, have a conflict with Grampa who doesn't understand the modern idea of giving children an allowance. Indeed there is an ongoing conflict over money. The family experiences its first tragedy when Grampa becomes seriously ill. On his deathbed Grampa asks his faithful wife, Sophie, to fulfill a strange and seemingly impossible promise.

You Can Take It with You

A Promise Is a Bond Sanctified by Trust

By Greta B. Lipson

Boris had worked desperately hard all of his life and was finally rewarded with a moderate sense of security. His little delicatessen prospered and Sophie and their grandchildren worked by his side after school and on weekends without a single complaint—except maybe once in a while when the children agitated for an allowance. It was clear to them that other children, who didn't work nearly as hard as they, got allowances, and it just wasn't fair!

The boys, Leon and Daniel, put up stock and waited on customers and even little sister Becky could make change and do odds and ends to keep things in order. When they approached their grandfather, he would say, "Have I told you about the Great Depression, when grown men were selling apples on the street for a nickel apiece and people were digging into garbage cans to find something to eat?"

And the children would answer patiently, "Yes, Grampa. We heard about the Great Depression."

"Did you know that we were so poor that all we could afford was to rent a bedroom with kitchen privileges from the Allegretti family?"

Leon, the oldest, was the most realistic and the most resigned, "I told you guys to forget it," he advised his brother and sister. "Grampa never heard about allowances in his whole entire life. So forget the allowance, 'cause he's never going to say yes. It means nothing for me, nothing for you, Daniel, and nothing for Becky."

"He's stingy," the two youngest muttered, "That's all there is to it. That's his biggest problem." They had it all figured out.

When their grandmother, Sophie, heard them, she always defended her husband staunchly. "Your grandfather doesn't understand why children should get money for doing what they are supposed to do for the family. That's not the way he grew up! Maybe you don't understand the way he feels. Maybe you can't understand because you've always had it so good. Someday when you grow up you'll see what it's like to struggle to make a living."

"But, Grandma," they whined.

"That's enough already. I don't want to hear anymore. When you get older you'll appreciate what he's done for you." She had heard enough.

"But Grandma, I don't get it."

"You don't have to get it," she scolded. "Just respect your grandfather."

Very soon after, the children and Sophie were overwhelmed with sadder and more important matters. Boris fell gravely ill and the course of his sickness was quick and relentless.

The family hovered at his bedside. This was the first test of their strength as the children, in a frightened huddle, listened to the hushed conversation between their grandparents. Sophie held her husband's waxen, cold hand. He whispered to his wife in a failing voice, "I have one final favor to ask of you."

"Anything you want," she replied softly.

"Will you promise first, Sophie, before I ask you?"

"I have never broken a promise to you, Boris, through all our years together." Sophie leaned toward his face with loving concern.

Boris's voice weakened. He seemed strangely disconnected from them but focused all his strength on this moment. As if from a remote place they heard him say, "I want you to promise that you will bury me with all my money."

There was a horrified silence. The children froze with the portent of Grampa's last request. The security of their future would be dashed to pieces on the whim of this strange, sick man who was their grandfather. Suspended in time, they looked into their grandmother's impassive face and, disbelieving, they heard her say, "I promise you faithfully, my husband, to honor your last request. Now rest."

Boris closed his eyes in serene contentment and left them for his eternal sleep. The children wept near hysteria—partly over the loss of their grandfather and partly over the immensity of Sophie's promise to him. "Oh, Grandma," they wailed, "how could you do this? Why did you agree to make such a promise? What will happen to us now?"

"It was your grandfather's deathbed wish. There will be no further discussion." They knew her heart was breaking, but her face was stone.

"But you won't do it will you, Grandma? You wouldn't bury him with his money? Sophie's silence was her only reply to the children.

The funeral was small and Malkivich's Funeral Home was adequate to the occasion. Neighborhood friends came and some old-time customers from the delicatessen. The eulogy was brief and respectful. It would have been a fitting service for any of the hardworking people in the community.

It was time for the ritual to end. The casket was to be closed after the family said their last good-byes. Leon was the tallest, and he could see his grandmother, strong and loyal to the last, as she walked to the casket to look at her husband's face for one final time. Daniel and Becky held hands tightly; all three children were watchful and disbelieving. Sophie bent over the casket. Tenderly she touched Boris's fingers folded piously over his chest. With the tolerance and understanding borne of many years of companionship, she fulfilled her promise to the dead man. She pressed into his clasped palms a personal check made out in the full amount of their hard-earned savings.

You Can Take It with You

Point of View–Discussion Questions

1. Did Sophie keep her promise to Boris, or did she break her promise? (Remember that she wrote out a check in the full amount of their life savings.)

Possible Answer

Sophie kept her promise by leaving a check in the casket which represented the full amount of their life savings. Among the living, a check is regarded as a legitimate form of financial transaction. A check is a written order to a bank to pay the stated amount of money from one's bank account. Clearly, Boris could neither cash a check nor could he spend any money as a dead man! Sophie promised to "honor" her husband's request. What is more—she gave comfort to a dying man who, for whatever reason, wanted to take his money with him to the grave.

2. Are there some kinds of promises which should be more binding than others—or is a promise a promise no matter what it involves? Expand on this.

3. Why does money cause conflict in families? How is it possible that both too much and not enough money can cause problems?

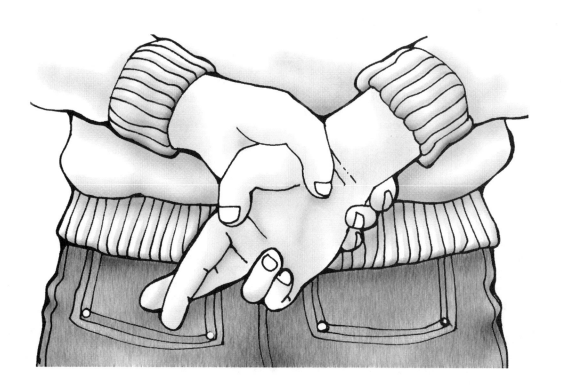

You Can Take It with You

Improvisation–Role Play Variations

1. Play the deathbed scene or any other scene with dramatic possibilities which help to amplify some of the issues in the story.

2. In several groups, work on skits entitled "But You Promised!" Present a variety of episodes that will demonstrate reasons for breaking promises. The choice may be from the serious to the sublime. Which promises would be the most forgivable to break (if any)? Consider parents and their promises to their children.

3. Select two opposing teams to present persuasive speeches on

   - "Money Brings Trouble"
   - "Money Brings Responsibility"

   Speakers should try to convince the audience to accept their team's point of view. Discuss any issues that were presented by any of the team members which were significant.

You Can Take It with You

Writing Suggestions

1. What is so important about a promise between family members, friends, or associates? State the reasons for your point of view. Based upon your opinion, do you believe that Sophie's actions were honorable or dishonorable?

2. In Mark Twain's *Adventures of Tom Sawyer*, there is a different approach to the topic of promises. "To promise not to do a thing is the surest way in the world to make a body want to go out and do that very thing." In a paragraph write an explanation of this from your own personal experience.

3. In a newspaper article in *The Detroit Free Press* Ellen Creager wrote, "Being poor and feeling poor are two different things." Explain that point of view. Would a rich person or a poor person make that statement? What did she mean?

Name _____

You Can Take It with You

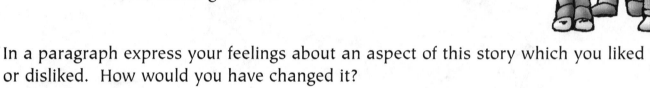

A Promise Is a Bond Sanctified by Trust
Student Comment

Characters: Boris, grandfather   Daniel, middle grandson
                 Sophie, grandmother   Becky, granddaughter
                 Leon, oldest grandson

In a paragraph express your feelings about an aspect of this story which you liked or disliked. How would you have changed it?

Alternative: Now that the story has been discussed, explain the proverb above from your point of view.

_____

_____

_____

_____

_____

_____

_____

_____

_____

_____

_____

_____

Chapter 3
Sand Art, on Deadline

Sand Art, on Deadline

Synopsis

Mike Angelo, a sculptor, goes to the seashore with all his sculpting equipment and over a period of several hours begins to build a majestic castle of sand. The passing crowd is drawn by the power of his talent as he creates medieval doorways flanked by U-shaped towers, elaborate systems of bridges and gates, battlements, and spiral staircases. The beach people begin to form a large, appreciative audience who are captured by the romance of his work. When Angelo completes the last refinements on this miniaturized masterpiece, the crowd is enthralled and then dumfounded by what follows.

Sand Art, on Deadline*
Talent Is a Divine Gift—
Not to Be Squandered

Anonymous

The young man arrived on the Massachusetts beach early carrying a portable radio, a shovel, and an odd assortment of tools. There were a bricklayer's trowel, a palette knife, spatulas, spoons, and a spray bottle.

He walked down near the water—the tide was out—put down the radio and tuned it to soft rock. Then he shoveled wet sand into a pile nearly four feet high and as many feet across. He took up the trowel and used it to slice large hunks off the pile, creating a rectangular shape.

After that, he set to work with palette knife, spatulas and spoons. He shaped a graceful tower, topped walls with crenelated battlements, fashioned elegant bay windows, and carved out a massive front gate.

The man knew his sand. With deft strokes, he smoothly finished some surfaces, embroidered baroque designs on others. As delicate shapes began to dry, he gently moistened them with water from the spray bottle, lest they crumble in the breeze.

All this took hours. People gathered, commenting to each other and asking questions of the sculptor. Lost in concentration, he gave only perfunctory replies. At last he stood back, apparently satisfied with a castle worthy of the Austrian countryside or Disneyland.

Then he gathered his tools and radio and moved them up to drier sand. He had known for a while what many in the rapt crowd still overlooked; the tide was coming in. Not only had he practiced his craft with confidence and style, he had done so against a powerful, immutable deadline.

As the spectators looked on, water began to lap at the base of the castle. In minutes it was surrounded, a miniature Mont-Saint-Michel.

Then the rising flood began to erode the base, chunks of wall fell, the tower tumbled, finally the gate's arch collapsed. More minutes passed, and small waves erased bay windows and battlements—soon no more than a modest lump was left.

Many in the crowd looked distraught; some voiced dismay. But the sculptor remained serene. He had, after all, had a wonderful day, making beauty out of nothing, and watching it return to nothing as time and tide moved on.

*Copyright 1989 by The New York Times Company. Reprinted by permission. Sunday, August 13, 1989, Section 22E.

Sand Art, on Deadline

Ephemeral Art

The word *ephemeral* means "something that lasts for a very brief time." There are expressions in art and other pursuits that can be described as ephemeral like the sand castle fashioned on the beach, which we all knew would only last until the tide came in and swept it all away. The most popular of these pursuits among children all over the world is face painting. See it now—wash it off later!

What forms can you think of that can be described as ephemeral? The faces of funny clowns at the circus, too, are a good example which is washed off at the end of a performance. T-shirts, bumper stickers, cake decorations, ice sculptures, snowmen, wild hair fashions, flower arrangements, pavement chalk art—are all creative expressions that disappear quickly or over a measured length of time.

Sand Art, on Deadline
Rube Goldberg

Rube Goldberg (1883-1970) was a wildly ingenious cartoonist who won the prestigious Pulitzer Prize. He helps us appreciate that art is expressed in many forms and uses a great variety of materials! The Rube Goldberg Machine Competitions continue to take place in high schools and colleges of engineering annually all over the country to this very day. There are rules for constructing the working apparatus—but the critical guideline is that a very simple task is performed by an incredibly, complicated "artful" machine! Organize a group of your classmates to dream up a Rube Goldberg machine. Visit the library or get online to see these inventions and how they function. Think "cracking an egg" in countless mechanical steps!

Sand Art, on Deadline

For the Teacher

Here is another twist to the end of the sand castle story which demonstrates that not all people who build castles in the sand are drifters, dreamers or leisure time artisans!

In California there is a unique enterprise which sells sand sculpting, to order. The castles (and other scenes) are constructed to be used as a promotional lure to attract crowds to shopping malls, conventions, and special events of all kinds. The structures, further described in the brochure of *Sand Sculptors International*, are remarkable in their grandeur and accuracy:

> "Todd Vander Pluym and his SSI staff are not only the current U.S. Open, World, and International Sand Sculpture Champions, but they also hold all current world records for sand sculpture. SSI artisans, supervised by Todd, have been creating sand sculpture for more than 40 years. Todd is an architect by training, an artist by design and a sculptor by desire. He holds more than 160 sand sculpture championships including 4 world championships and 6 U.S. Open championships."

Sand sculpture is described in this literature as "The Ultimate Promotion." And so we have a double twist on a story when we are later informed that building things out of sand has been turned into a profit-making business by some people with extraordinary vision and enterprise. As immigrants to our shores would say, "Only in America!"

Sand Art, on Deadline
Point of View—Discussion Questions

1. Why would a talented person such as Mike Angelo, the sculptor, put hard work into a creative project and be willing to see it disappear or be destroyed irretrievably by time and the elements?

   Possible Answer

   Perhaps Mike Angelo, the artist, had hardly been able to sell his art, and the financial return was not worth the cost of his materials. But more importantly he realized that his greatest fulfillment was in the genuine pleasure he experienced in the process of making his sculpture. His castle was an expression of his talent and his interest in working with sand as a medium. This fact was more important to him than profit or recognition.

2. Some people think that creative women and men in the arts have a gift which they should share with others. First, they believe that those with talent have an obligation to the future. Secondly, they believe that the work of such artists should be created to endure as part of human history and as a chronicle of the times. Another point of view holds that talent belongs to the fortunate few, and it is theirs to use as they please. If some artists choose to create works that do not last for future enjoyment, there are those who believe that is the artist's decision and no one else's business. What do you believe?

3. What would the world be like if nothing was handed down in the arts, the sciences, or in technology? How would it be to reinvent the wheel with every new generation? What are the implications of having no previous information to draw on from the past? What do our achievements owe to the past in all fields of endeavor?

4. Theodore Dreiser, an American novelist (1871-1945), described the arts as "The stored honey of the human soul, gathered on wings . . . ." How would you explain that quote?

Sand Art, on Deadline

Improvisation–Role Play Variations

1. Role-play the sand castle event on the beach from the standpoint of four or five observers and a narrator as if it were a sporting event. Improvise a running commentary describing the audience, the scene, and the construction of this magnificent structure.

2. As a TV newscaster, interview some of the observers at the seashore who were shocked when the tide came in and gouged out huge chunks of Mike Angelo's stunning work. Some people know Mike from "around" and have strong views on his art and his personality. Some think he's a genius; others say he's just a beach bum with an oversized ego. There is a group who believe that anyone who puts in so much effort for nothing must be a little crazy.

3. Conduct a committee meeting of the National Endowment for the Arts. Your group has funds to appropriate to worthy artists in your community of Anytown. There are different points of view among the members regarding the worthiness of certain works of art and disagreement about which artists deserve some support for their creative endeavors. Some of you like representational art and consider modern art as junk. Others dislike traditional art but strongly prefer works with a modern perspective. Express your standards for awarding grant money. Will you be big enough to give grant money to someone with talent whose work you find to be disagreeable? Express the problems as you go along. What qualifies people to be on a committee which has the power to give out grant money from taxes? Should the committee members be experts on art or be watchdogs for the taxpayers?

Sand Art, on Deadline

Writing Suggestions

1. If, at this time, you could be an accomplished musician, artist, singer, sports figure, dancer, writer, or scientist, what would you choose to be and how important would it be to you to win the recognition and applause of the public? Would personal satisfaction be enough? Explain your attitude.

2. Yesterday you read in the newspaper that in November 1987, a painting by Vincent Van Gogh entitled *Irises* was sold at Sothebey's auction establishment in London, England, for 54 million dollars. The picture was not bought by an art lover but was bought as an investment. You know that the artist, Van Gogh, died sick and in poverty! Write a letter to the man who bought the picture. What is your reaction to the purchase and what would you say? Express your outrage, or dismay, or your admiration for the purchaser's keen business sense. How would the artist, Van Gogh, feel if he were to come back from the grave and hear about this purchase?

3. All art and folk art does not hang in museums. Included in this rich category are the comics which are a serious part of American mythology and a unique artistic expression. There is a highly individualized style to the characters and a special language that is demonstrated through the dialogue balloons. The art, the characterization, and the dialogue combine to impart a strong impression on the reader. Bring in your favorite comic strip and describe the qualities that you believe make it an effective artistic expression.

Name _____

Sand Art, on Deadline

Talent Is a Divine Gift—Not to Be Squandered
Student Comment

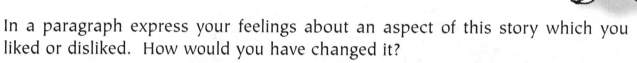

Characters: Mike Angelo, artist
                    Audience at the beach

In a paragraph express your feelings about an aspect of this story which you liked or disliked. How would you have changed it?

Alternative: Now that the story has been discussed, explain the proverb above from your point of view.

_____

_____

_____

_____

_____

_____

_____

_____

_____

_____

_____

Chapter 4
The Blanket

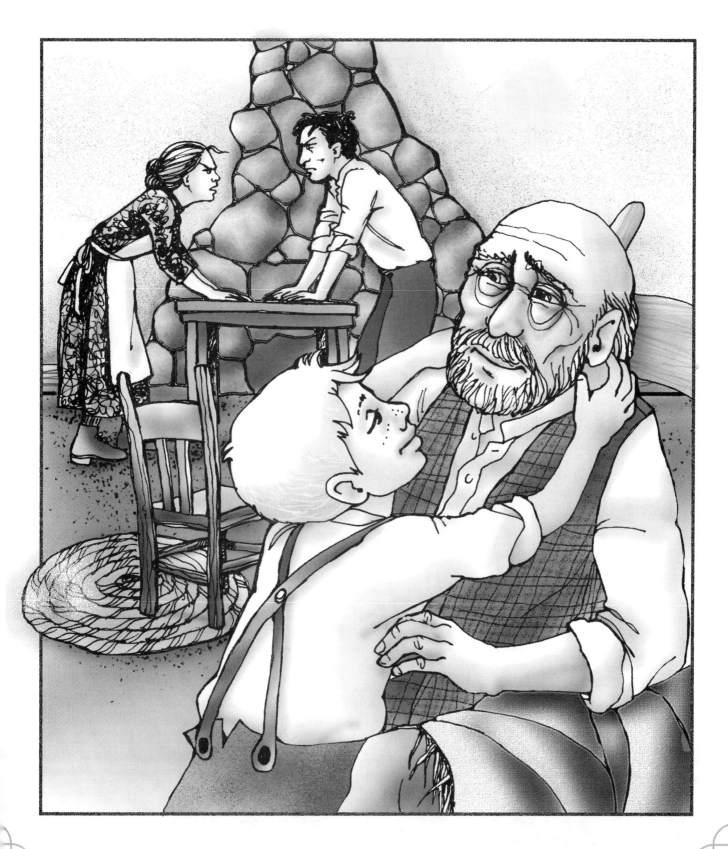

The Blanket*

Synopsis

Brendan O'Brien and his wife, Katy, are Irish tenant farmers who live with their little boy Sean and with Grampa who is dearly loved by his grandson. Because they are desperately poor, Sean's mother and father are always searching for ways to survive their impoverished existence. One day Brendan and Katy decide upon a solution which seems hard-hearted and unconscionable. Just as they are about to act on this plan, their son, Sean, makes a suggestion that has shattering implications for their own future.

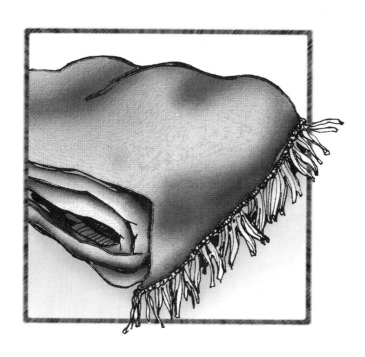

*Retold by Greta B. Lipson, Ed.D. from *Favorite Folktales from Around the World*, edited by Jane Yolen (New York: Random House, 1986).

The Blanket

We Reap as We Have Sown

Retold by Greta B. Lipson

Perhaps there were other poor people in the county, but none of the tenant farmers were poorer than Brendan O'Brien and his wife, Katy. Their young son, Sean, was a happy child, oblivious to the hardships and the grinding poverty suffered by his parents and his grandfather. He was always at play—curious and acutely alert to everything around him on the farm.

Every day was an experience of discovery for Sean and his questions never stopped. But the O'Briens were far too worn out at the end of the day from working their small farm to have any patience left for the little boy. Besides—there were real problems that compounded their constant struggle. Brendan reminded his wife, "The rent is due soon, Katy, and we've put very little by to pay the landlord."

"Too many mouths to feed here," she grumbled in response.

Only Grampa had the patience to answer Sean's questions. The old man had lived with them since Sean was an infant, working the farm side by side with the young family. Finally age had bent his bones, and he was not strong enough to keep up the hard labor. But none of this mattered to Sean, who only cared that his grampa was his very best companion. For every question Sean asked, the old man had an answer embedded in an elaborate story. He told about Celtic tribes who came from the island of Great Britain, and he told about the Viking raiders who invaded the east and south coasts of Ireland.

Then Grampa would spin a geography lesson and say, "There were the first towns of Ireland and they'd be Cork and Dublin, Limerick and Waterford" And Sean listened, loving their time together.

Slowly the joyous days began to wane and there filtered in a dismal overlay in the atmosphere of the small cottage. Sean grew aware of a mood of misery that surfaced with more arguments over the dinner table. It was the only time the small family sat down together, and the sound of the same ugly refrain was heard over and over again. He had heard it all before but he began to listen carefully to try to understand the cause.

"Too many mouths to feed in this house. If we could trim down the food and drink we might be able to save some money." Sean's mother, Katy, seemed to have a better understanding of expenses and management than his father. Clearly money was at the root of the problem.

As far as Sean could tell, his father, Brendan, resisted the litany of complaints that came from his mother. Brendan would only say, "But Katy—he's my very own father!" His brow would furrow and make a dark line that marked his face with brooding.

Through all of this the grandfather seemed not to hear. He grew quieter through the miserable winter days and nights. They talked around him as if he did not exist. There was no more telling of stories for Sean and sometimes at the table, when the surly exchange would begin between his parents, the boy noticed that something would come over Grampa's eyes—an opaque glaze—as if he were turned inward, listening to distant voices, perhaps kinder and more bearable. The old man's head was bowed more, and he would look down as if to study the food in his dinner bowl. When he finished eating, he was careful not to move until the others left the table. It was as if he did not wish to remind them that he was present in the room.

Then it happened on a day when they were all in the house huddled against the outside weather—sullen and silent. "Now is as good a time as any," Katy O'Brien told her husband. She was sharp and angry with him—but that is the way she was these days.

"Does it have to be today?" Brendan asked.

"This is as good a day as you'll get," she said—her voice rising, insistent, determined.

All at once Sean understood. The solution to their desperation would be to have one less mouth to feed. Grampa was to be turned out to fend for himself. Together, Brendan and Katy took the old man by his elbow, lifting him out of his chair. He was quiet as death. He did not protest. Somehow they had prepared him for this—their last act of filial responsibility, and he knew it was coming.

Sean saw his grandfather being moved toward the door—a sleepwalker in a painful dream, about to be cast out into an uncertain future. Katy hesitated. She spoke. "Here, let's give him a blanket off the bed." Briskly—with no motion wasted—she turned toward the cot nearest the fireplace and swept the blanket off the bed. She wrapped it around his poor rounded shoulders—and made of him a pathetic bundle of a human being.

"Wait, Mother!" her little son shouted. "Just give him half a blanket, I beg of you.

"But why?" his parents asked in shocked surprise over their son's interference.

"Please give Grampa half a blanket—then I will have something to give to you both when it's my time to turn you out."

The Blanket

Point of View—Discussion Questions

1. What values in our culture give this story its impact? What is there in the conclusion that is personally upsetting to some readers?

    Possible Answer

    Our social code teaches us to honor our parents and to be responsible for those we love. The ending is disturbing because of the inhumanity of turning out an elderly and vulnerable human being. The profound effect is introduced by the little boy, Sean, who has witnessed the example his parents have set. His statement makes it clear that the same miserable fate of abandonment waits for his mother and father, and Sean will be the one to carry on this treachery against them. On a purely selfish level, the events suggest that the same thing could happen to any one of us when we are old and helpless.

2. In the context of this story, how do you explain this proverb: "What goes around comes around"? What evidence is there that this statement is true or false? How would justice be done if the proverb were true? Explain the following: "Be to your parents such a one as you would pray your children be to you." (Attributed to Isocrates, a great Greek orator 436–338 B.C.)

3. Given the poverty and desperation of Brendan and Katy O'Brien, what other course of action could they have followed to solve their money problems? What realistic advice could you give to these poor Irish tenant farmers? Is it true that some human problems have no solutions?

The Blanket

Improvisation–Role Play Variations

1. Play the scene in the home of Brendan and Katy O'Brien, just as it reads, when Grampa is about to be turned out of the house. Extend the dialogue between Sean and his parents to whatever point the actors choose. Mr. and Mrs. O'Brien believe they are doing the only thing they can to help them survive.

2. Grampa and his grandson, Sean, discuss a plan to run away together. They try to analyze the difficulties of supporting themselves and explore the possibilities of an old man and a child earning enough money to survive. They are motivated by their companionship and love for one another.

3. The old man discovers the plan to turn him out. He prefers to retain his dignity and leave the O'Brien household voluntarily. In time Grampa becomes a beloved and financially successful storyteller who travels over the entire country. Brendan and Katy arrange a meeting with him. He agrees but is certain that they are in financial need and that is their only reason for having communicated with him. What happens at the meeting?

The Blanket

Writing Suggestions

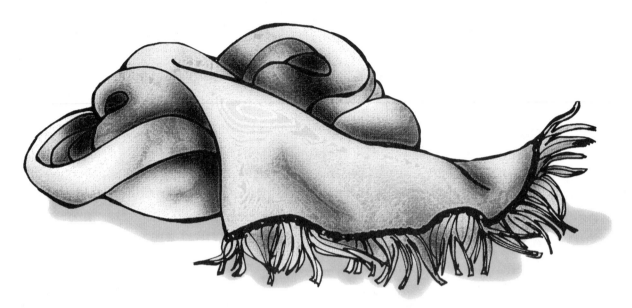

1. Write a paragraph describing specific ways in which senior citizens are able to help young people. Think about schools, community centers, hospitals, and places of business. Research grandparent surrogate programs. What important function do such programs provide for adults and young people alike?

2. The Social Security system in our country is the only source of income for many retired old people. Research the details of this program and explain its benefits in a paragraph. All American citizens are affected by this program; in which we all have Social Security numbers. From what you understand, how much are these monthly payments and is the amount enough to live on currently? How does a senior citizen survive who has no family, no support system, and can no longer earn a living?

3. There is a large organization called The American Association of Retired Persons (AARP) which publishes a magazine called *Modern Maturity*. Find a copy in your local public library and review its contents. List the issues in which older citizens are interested. What are their political and social concerns? Why should this make any difference to you?

4. Describe an older member of your family or someone who is a family friend. If you project into the future, what kind of an old person do you imagine you will be? What do you hope to do in your advanced years?

Name _____

The Blanket

We Reap as We Have Sown
Student Comment

Characters: Sean, the little boy
              Brendan and Katy O'Brien, his parents
              Grampa

In a paragraph express your feelings about an aspect of this story which you liked or disliked. How would you have changed it?

Alternative: Now that the story has been discussed, explain the proverb above from your point of view.

_____

_____

_____

_____

_____

_____

_____

_____

_____

_____

_____

_____

Mrs. Esposito's Pizza

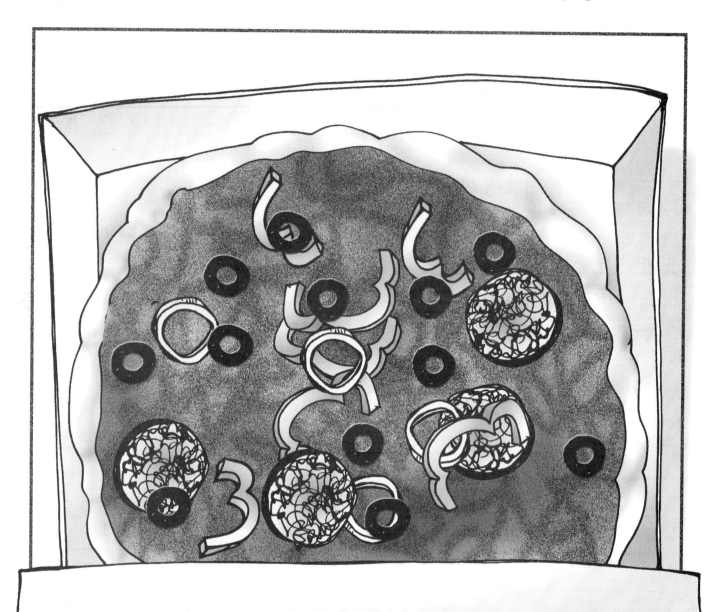

Mrs. Esposito's Pizza
Synopsis

Victor is a rich dude with gold chains, sharp clothes and all the outward signs of financial success. He has clearly overcome his poor beginnings as he wheels his big car back to his old slum neighborhood to buy one of Mrs. Esposito's pizzas. Swaggering into the restaurant, he gives his careful order, all the while happy and high spirited with the prospect of his luscious supper. Victor leaves the store with a big steaming pizza in hand. The unexpected turn of events leaves Victor half dead with fright and bewilderment!

Mrs. Esposito's Pizza

Things Are Seldom What They Seem

By Greta B. Lipson

Victor was always comfortable going back to his old neighborhood. He never made it a secret that he grew up there—indeed it was his badge of honor. In no way was he ashamed of his humble beginnings nor was he embarrassed about his determined trip out of the place. As a matter of fact he now felt inordinate pride over his present status. He loved being rich and successful.

Victor couldn't explain it, but there was always this need to go back to the streets of his youth. Perhaps it reaffirmed his authenticity and made him a better person—one whose affluence had not spoiled him. Victor was fond of saying, "You can take the boy out of the slum, but you can't take the slum out of the boy!"

The familiar sights were reassuring to him. Of course there were some changes over the years—but many of the store fronts were just as he remembered them. He relished the pungent smells, the ragtag people, the jumbled merchandise, the sounds and the spicy ethnic treats! Unlike the way he lived as a deprived child, he was now able to buy absolutely anything that appealed to his palate. That fact of life was a lasting joy to his stomach. No more unfulfilled yearning for him! He could afford to have it all.

The daily newspaper had made a big thing about developers who were gentrifying the neighborhood—making it more attractive for the young professionals who were moving in. But he wasn't worried about any serious inroads into the look and feel of the place. The new residents would surely consider it important to protect the old "flavor" of the streets and the shops. They would glory in its vintage, and it would forever be his old neighborhood.

Easing his Mercedes against the curb in a clearly marked "No Parking" zone, Victor began to review mentally the tasty choices which would appear on the menu over the backboard. Double pepperoni? Absolutely! Anchovies! Too salty—but they made the thirst-quenching soda pop so acutely delicious. Olives? You said it! He imagined black olives looking up at him like cartoon circles unblinking in a sea of bubbly, aromatic tomato sauce. As usual his choice would be an Esposito's Special. His stomach was sending messages to his brain which was generating even more fantasies. He rehearsed the very first slice of pizza—cut adrift in space—separated from its crispy moorings. He envisioned warm attenuated strings of mozzarella cheese hanging on—then disengaged—finally finding their way up to his eager lips.

It always happened this way, and it never ceased to amaze him that thoughts of food could cause a rush of saliva. He was like one of Pavlov's psychologically conditioned dogs. All it took was one thought of the pizza, and a great surge of saliva filled his mouth in readiness for the feast.

Once inside Esposito's, he gave the deliberate order of an aficionado and hung over the counter longingly. He would play a time game with himself while he waited patiently for the oven to give up its wondrous baked delight. Finally the pizza was pulled from the hearth, was lovingly dusted with hot peppers, and was packaged. Victor smelled that fragrance which was at once a mix of an oregano cloud and a hot cardboard box.

Almost at the very moment he stepped out of the store he felt a presence behind him. "Stop right there, Bozo, and don't even think about turning around!" He clutched his outsize pizza box as if he were a rigid sentry standing watch.

Victor felt an insistent, unmistakable object thrust painfully into his ribs. A gun. Somebody was actually holding him up in front of a busy pizza joint. Where was everybody at supper time anyway? He had heard stories about the physical sensations people experienced when in a state of fright. Can you really vomit on an empty stomach, he wondered? He repressed a whimper but was horrified when a pathetic sound escaped.

"Whaja say?" His assailant was anxious. Then, not waiting for an answer, the guy with the gun threatened, "Just shuddup, Bozo."

A beseeching voice came out of Victor's throat. "You can take anything I've got," he ventured. Was that piping voice actually his? He couldn't control it as it rambled on.

The snickered response was predictable. "Don't need no lip from you, Bozo."

Victor quickly inventoried the worldly goods on his body: a Count Dulane leather coat, a serpentine gold chain around his neck, a diamond initial ring, and his brand-new imported watch. That watch was his baby, his status symbol. Its weight pressed heavily—conspicuously as it glimmered on his wrist. He clung to the pizza as a toddler to its blanket—the warmth of it heating his numbed belly.

The rest happened quickly. With a dancer's grace the mugger pulled the gun out of Victor's ribs, did an astonishing pirouette, whirled in front of him and looked into Victor's eyes, full face. With one brutal wrench, the thug tore at Victor's frozen hands, whipped his wrists and pulled away his prize. He took off down the street at breakneck speed with coattails flying—like a western duster on a frontier bad guy. The hapless Victor watched, disbelieving, as the hoodlum disappeared from sight like a phantom streak.

Shaken almost insensible from fright, Victor lurched in a half faint, dropping to the pavement on one knee. The curb broke his fall and gave him meager comfort as he sat with his head buried in his arms. He sobbed uncontrollably. "Oh thank you, thank you, God!" he slobbered, "I can't believe it! I'm still alive. That idiot left everything I had worth stealing, and all he took was my pizza!"

Mrs. Esposito's Pizza

Point of View—Discussion Questions

1. Is the mugger less a thief for having stolen a pizza worth a few dollars instead of robbing Victor of his watch or gold chain which were worth a fortune?

   Possible Answer

   The legal definition of *larceny* means "taking away someone else's property unlawfully with the intention of permanently depriving the owner of its use." The legal definition of *robbery means* "taking property from a person by force or fear." Either way, the law regards the theft of the pizza as a crime. However, a judge or a prosecutor or a jury would probably take into account the value of the object taken.

2. A *misdemeanor* is defined as "a minor crime usually punishable by less than one year in jail and/or a fine." What factor is there in this incident that would make it more serious? (The use of a gun makes this a crime of armed robbery, which is a felony. The law considers crimes of violence against people more serious than crimes against property.)

3. Why do you think someone would risk the possible penalty of armed robbery, if convicted, just to grab something to eat? What is the reason that people commit crimes in general? Statistics indicate that more crimes are committed by young people than by older people. What would you say are the reasons for this?

4. Where would you go if you were homeless and needed a meal to keep body and soul together? Are there soup kitchens and shelters available in your city to feed and house children and adults who are homeless? Who sponsors and supports these places?

Mrs. Esposito's Pizza

Improvisation–Role Play Variations

1. A television reporter has been alerted by a "Neighborhood Watch" group about Victor's mugging. The reporter is on the scene and is interviewing the owner of the pizza parlor, Mrs. Esposito, and others. The neighbors express strong feelings about Victor, whom they regard as a show-off who was asking for trouble. Mrs. Esposito disagrees with them vigorously and is very vocal about it.

2. The mugger has been apprehended and is at the police station. An attorney, Mr. Loophole, has been appointed by the court to represent him. They are in a private room discussing the mugger's defense. What is he telling the attorney about his motives and what actually occurred? How could you make him a sympathetic character despite the charges against him?

3. An argument occurs in the old neighborhood among the residents regarding Victor and his attitudes. Some claim that Victor doesn't have a social conscience because he turned his back on them and their problems and moved away. Since he acquired money he has no interest whatever in their difficulties. The neighbors claim that if he cared about them he would be involved constructively in the community. Victor replies by saying that moving upward and out is what America is all about. He thinks they are all unfair.

Mrs. Esposito's Pizza

Writing Suggestions

1. Describe something upsetting that has happened to you. How could you have avoided the incident by making other choices or decisions about your actions? If you had no control over what happened, did the event occur because you were in the wrong place at the wrong time? Did poor judgment or fate play a role in the happening?

2. What personal possessions do you value which have great meaning to you but would have little or no monetary value to anyone else? Explain the sentiment that is involved with this item.

3. Based upon the characterization of Victor in the story, what was your impression of the kind of person he was? Did your attitude toward him affect your feelings about him as a victim? Write a statement.

4. Based upon the characterization of Victor in the story, what was your impression of the kind of person he was? Did your attitude toward him affect your feelings about him as a victim? Write a statement.

Mrs. Esposito's Pizza

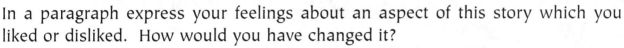

Things Are Seldom What They Seem
Student Comment

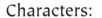

Characters: Victor   Mrs. Esposito, restaurant owner
              A mugger   Neighbors

In a paragraph express your feelings about an aspect of this story which you liked or disliked. How would you have changed it?

Alternative: Now that the story has been discussed, explain the proverb above from your point of view.

_____

_____

_____

_____

_____

_____

_____

_____

_____

_____

_____

_____

_____

_____

Chapter 6
Bon Appetit

Bon Appetit
Synopsis

Felix, a waitperson at the Continental Restaurant, serves an extraordinary piece of pastry to an old friend, and customer, who has just gone off a diet. The dessert was created by the newly arrived chef, Emmanuel LaLenter, and it proves to be a wildly successful culinary achievement. The dieter, an amateur cook, is determined to get the recipe by any means necessary—fair or foul—with Felix acting as coconspirator! The deed is done but the revelation is unspeakable!

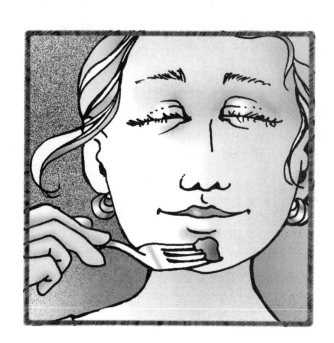

Bon Appetit

What You Don't Know Won't Hurt You

By Greta B. Lipson

I'm not one of those selfish, secretive people who refuses to share a recipe—but I worked so hard to get this one and risked so much that I'm not sure the goddess of cooking and baking would allow me to hand it out.

It all happened a few weeks ago, when I had just gone off one of my many diets and felt that I deserved a treat worthy of my good behavior. After all those painful months of deprivation—right or wrong—I was determined to make this a reward to remember. My friends don't call me "El-Blimpo" for nothing. But the truth is that I would rather starve for two days and then splurge my calories on a gastronomic joy than eat a barnful of bran and a bale of hay because it's good for me.

The word on the street was that there was a new chef at the Continental who made pastries one could die for! His name was Emmanuel LaLenter, and he was everything one would expect from a world-class chef, which translated means he was arrogant, temperamental, and impossible to get along with. But how those customers slavered over his creations. The patrons were extravagant with praise.

I, too, was one of those manic customers dying to try LaLenter's delight, and I showed up at the Continental Restaurant as soon as I could get there. Felix, the waitperson, knew me as a steady customer with a fatal weakness for desserts. Besides that he understood that I was an adventuresome amateur cook who loved to turn out luscious dishes to feed to my friends. When I sat down, Felix came over in a flash. We were good old buddies, and he knew I was there because my penance was over.

"You heard already, right?" He smiled his best smile reserved for the people who understood really fine food. We were kindred souls. Felix served excellent cuisine with pride, and I obliged by eating it with passion!

"I'm not here for dinner, Felix. I'm here with a clean and highly tuned palate for just one single dish that this LaLenter fellow makes. In experienced and wise judgment, what is his foremost achievement in pastry?"

He warmed to my question and, looking upward, seemed to be searching for the answer on the ceiling. I knew better than to make smart remarks at a time like this. He was giving my question serious consideration and was to be respected! I was silent and patient. He finally responded, "My recommendation to you for a first adventure is LaLenter's Black Satin Pie paved with chantilly cream."

"Are you suggesting something as homely as pie? All-American pie? Not 'haute cuisine'?" I asked timidly.

Felix didn't take kindly to my reaction, "Don't insult me. Would I steer you wrong? Have I ever disappointed you?"

Everything was in readiness: the fine china, the damask napkin, the single rose in the bud vase, a carafe of aromatic coffee, and a chilled dessert fork. I sat expectantly, like a greedy child. Felix set the wedge of Black Satin Pie in front of me. Oh joy and perfection. The presentation was glorious and uncluttered. Only a single strawberry dipped in white chocolate sat at the side of the plate. A perky green stem poked out through the swirls of chocolate.

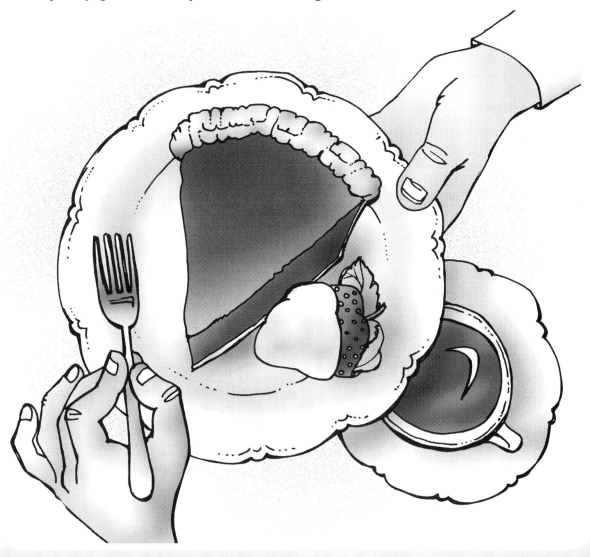

Black Satin was an implosion on my palate, all gloriously creamy in bittersweet chocolate triumph. I felt my eyelids flutter in the ecstasy of the moment. The nut-like crust was sinfully delicate, unlike anything I had ever experienced before. Filling and crust were wedded in a swooning combination made richer by the billowing chantilly cream—sweetened with a subtle, aromatic orange honey. The eating was slow. When I was finished I sat, as if in a reverie, looking at the empty plate.

Whatever I had to do to unlock the recipe of Black Satin Pie—I was prepared to do. Felix was my only hope. Remember that he talks the language of good food, but he is not interested in creating it. To want to produce a culinary creation in one's own kitchen, you must be moved by a compelling lust to cook. What is more, you must enjoy listening to the admiring approval from your eaters who make subvocal, primitive sounds meaning "I have fallen madly in love with your food!"

I cajoled and threatened Felix and in a challenging test of our friendship, he copied the secret recipe from LaLenter's private file. I was thrilled—but there was one more very serious obstacle for me. How in the world did he make that heavenly flaky pastry with its intricate scalloped edge?

Felix couldn't find any evidence of the recipe in the file. "But I do have a suggestion," he said, warming to the task. "Why don't you pretend that you are going to use the phone next to the back door of the kitchen? The door there has a perfect porthole window to watch through. LaLenter's pastry table is right by the door, and you'll have a good view of everything he does. Make sure you come in the late morning when the deliveries are over. That's just about the time he gets started on his fancy baking. And for heaven's sake, watch out for his assistant, Big Jenny. She watches over him protectively, like a bear with a cub. Have no doubt that she would probably kill you if she knew what you were up to!"

The hallway was dark near the kitchen door and I was there, slightly scared because I could hear Big Jenny hollering orders to the staff. My eyes grew accustomed to the dim light, and I watched as LaLenter prepared his nine-inch (22.86 cm) pie plates for the pastry. The pie shells were made from a water-whisk recipe which I had never seen before, but I was more interested in the cute, kinky crimped edge he designed at the rim of the crust. He rolled out the dough expertly. As I watched him, I went through the steps in my mind. Easy now. Tear the waxed paper off the circle of dough. Dampen the rim of the pan so the shell won't shrink while it bakes. Fit it gently into the pie pan and now—start crimping the edge.

LaLenter didn't lose a motion as he pulled his big, ugly false teeth out of his mouth. I believe they were his uppers—plastic pink gums and all. At first I didn't understand what was happening. He didn't wipe the teeth off on his apron or anything. Instead he held them against the outside of the rim of dough on the pie pan. He pressed those fake choppers against the dough methodically and proceeded to push his thumb hard against the dough. The result was the cunning little pattern traced into the scalloped edge of the Black Satin piecrust that I had admired so much.

Fighting waves of nausea, I hung around just long enough to confirm that LaLenter trimmed all the pastry crusts in the same way. When he was through with his last creation, he popped those disgusting, discolored teeth back into his slack mouth like a demented genius. As for me—I was seriously sick for the rest of the day.

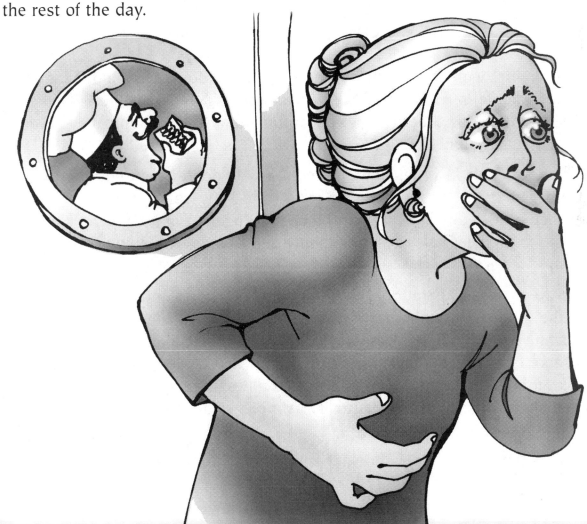

Bon Appetit

For the Teacher

Americans Love Pie!

When we first worked with this story in the classroom, everybody clamored for Chef Lalenter's recipe! First we had a show of hands: "Who likes pies?" we asked. All hands shot up! It was near lunchtime and the topic made everybody's mouth water.

We discussed our favorites and decided that you don't have to be a genius to make a pie. Then somebody had a great idea. Why don't we search out the pies each of us really like and put the recipes together in a class booklet! You can talk to the best bakers among family and friends who enjoy cooking and sharing.

Since we are not all great bakers, we decided on easy standards. That means that the guidelines are loose. If you prepare and roll out your own dough that's fine—if you use a frozen pre-prepared commercial crust, that's acceptable, too. If a graham cracker crust or chocolate cookie crumb crust is your choice, that will qualify as well. If you like cheesecake and it is prepared in a nine-inch *round* pan—that will qualify as a pie—just call it a cheesecake pie!

If you are ambitious (and we know you are), collect all the class recipes and assemble them in a yummy booklet entitled *Easy as Pie!*

Bon Appetit
For the Teacher

With great good luck, I met Mr. Brian Laurencelle, who is a master of quantity cookery and does not keep his recipes a secret! He prepares food for Boy Scout Troop 194 from Detroit in his role as the Food Service Director on Macinac Island Scout Service Camp in Michigan. With the help of an enthusiastic staff of three helpers, he cooks for 63 hungry scouts and their leaders following the traditions of their beloved favorites! Unlike some great cooks, Mr. Laurencelle was happy to share a traditional troop pie recipe that his scouts and leaders love to eat! And here it is!

Ice Cream Peanut Butter Pie

1. Buy or prepare a nine-inch graham cracker crust.

2. To prepare: Use $1\frac{1}{4}$ cups graham cracker crumbs.
   Melt $\frac{1}{3}$ cup butter or margarine.
   Mix crumb and butter well with a fork.
   Spread evenly in a pan and sides.
   Chill well in refrigerator.

3. To prepare filling: Cut one quart frozen vanilla ice cream in large chunks on a surface. Do not thaw.
   Take one cup peanut butter out of jar.

4. With a spatula, fold peanut butter through the ice cream cutting into small chunks.

5. Take a 12-ounce carton of thawed whipped topping and fold into ice cream.

6. Spread mixture into crust.

7. Refrigerate in deep freeze overnight. Make sure it is level.

8. To serve, take from freezer and slip onto a cutting board. With a very sharp knife, cut in half and then in reasonable portions. Drizzle some chocolate sauce on each slice with a strawberry or raspberry to make it look fancy. Enjoy!

Bon Appetit

Point of View—Discussion Questions

1. What would your local Board of Health think of the notion that "What you don't know won't hurt you"?

   Possible Answer

   The Board of Health is concerned with problems of public health in order to prevent and control the spread of disease. Communities are concerned with sanitation, contagious disease, immunization, animal bites, and other factors relative to the public well-being. Health codes and laws on local, state, and national levels are enforced to protect the population. Because the Board of Health does its utmost to educate and inform the population about good health practices, its philosophy would be, "What you don't know *can* hurt you."

2. Every semester history professor Milton Covensky of Wayne State University in Detroit would lecture to his students on two of his favorite topics. How would you define and explain the following?

   - The Tragedy of Ignorance (having no information or understanding of social and natural forces and events in life and therefore having no control)

   - The Tragedy of Knowledge (understanding and recognizing social and natural forces in life and being powerless to change the course of events)

   - Which of the above would you rather have?

3. What would you do if reporting Chef LaLenter's unsanitary kitchen practices were to put Felix's job in jeopardy? If you report someone for having done something seriously wrong, what could the consequences be? How does your relationship to that person affect your decision? Is there ever another way of dealing with a sticky situation aside from reporting it to the authorities? (Think about school situations.)

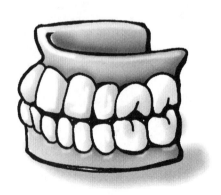

Bon Appetit

Improvisation—Role Play Variations

1. Pantomime the entire restaurant scene, as it reads, with the patron in ecstasy over the wonderful dessert. He wants to compliment everybody effusively—most especially Felix, the waitperson, and Emmanuel LaLenter, the pastry chef

2. Pantomime the entire restaurant scene, with a difficult patron who is incredibly dissatisfied with the service, the dessert, and almost everything. After a confrontation with the management and the help, the unhappy customer storms out of the restaurant

3. Assume the role of a Board of Health inspector assigned to Dirty Gertie's Homestyle Grill. With your clipboard in hand and Gertie at your elbow, how many and what kind of infractions do you encounter? Use your common sense as you discover one violation after another and complain out loud to Gertie about what you have found. Your disgust is obvious.

Bon Appetite
Writing Suggestions

1. Suppose that you were a consumer who had a complaint about a food product that was misrepresented in the advertisement. You are annoyed enough to write a letter of complaint to the manufacturer. Be specific and convincing with your disappointment in their product. How would you want them to improve on it, or do you want a refund?

2. Recall a delightful or a yucky experience you have had with strange food. Perhaps you ate an exotic dish and later discovered it was minced tongue, squid, sweetbread, or stuffed intestine. Where were you and how did it happen that you were eating something unfamiliar? Include the details.

3. How can food processors or manufacturers mislead the public? What would the motive be? Write a statement with your opinion. (Following this lead, do some research on the famous book, *The Jungle*, by Upton Sinclair, written almost 100 years ago in 1906. Remember that your Board of Health is a watchdog of the public health in your community! The book created a sensation because it exposed shocking conditions in the meat-packing industry. This information attracted the attention of President Theodore Roosevelt, who invited the author to the White House. The story generated public outrage and led to the passage of the Pure Food and Drug Act. What did the book reveal?)

Name _____

Bon Appetit

What You Don't Know Won't Hurt You
Student Comment

Characters:　The Dieter, a restaurant patron
　　　　　　　Felix, a waitperson
　　　　　　　Emmanuel LaLenter, the chef

In a paragraph express your feelings about an aspect of this story which you liked or disliked. How would you have changed it?

Alternative: Now that the story has been discussed, explain the proverb above from your point of view.

_____

_____

_____

_____

_____

_____

_____

_____

_____

_____

_____

_____

There's a Sucker Born Every Minute

There's a Sucker Born Every Minute*

Synopsis

Phil Flam, a con artist, goes into business selling Phil Flam's Famous Elixir which cures coughs, colds, sore moles, pimples on the belly, and asthma! He sells his miracle medicine from the contrived stage of his motorized prairie schooner at state fairs and special events. He is a man with a "silver tongue" who easily commands great crowds and a loyal following. One day Phil falls from the platform in a siege of acute illness as his concerned customers rush to his rescue. He has unwittingly set the stage for his own ignominious end.*

*Based upon an Aesop Fable, "The Shoemaker Turned Doctor."

There's a Sucker Born Every Minute

The Gullible Support the Sharpers

By Greta B. Lipson

There was this guy, Phil Flam, who sold shoes over in the general store in Grand Bend. Nobody could figure out how he did it, but his sales were phenomenal. He knew just what to say to people to charm them half senseless. It was a kind of intuition he had that never failed him. He was like the grand master of "folksy psychology," and he never even took a course. Matter of fact, this guy hardly went to school at all and had never graduated from grade 3.

His family had figured him for a bum who couldn't do much of anything. Seems like he never shut his mouth long enough to learn from his studies. His teacher had the same complaint. But everybody had to admit he talked really well—like a man with a silver tongue. Watching him operate at the shoe store was the best sport around. Flam had more moves than an octopus! When he saw a skinny self-conscious runt he'd say, "Hi there, Tiger. Still making hearts flutter among the pretty girls in town?" The runt would smile self-consciously and then seem to be just a little inflated by the joshing. (Flam was never a smart mouth. He was always believable.) But we all figured that Phil's snow jobs worked because people believe what they want to, even when it doesn't make a whole lot of sense.

If he was trying to sell to a tough guy he'd say, "I can tell that nobody puts anything over on you, and I'm not the one to try, but confidentially I want you to know . . . ." And then he'd say something conspiratorial to the fool who'd fall for it every time. Or else he'd say—like he was dying to know, "Can I ask you a personal question? Are you a weight lifter?"

When a young woman would come in with a testy attitude, Phil would move in real easy and say something like, "I know how it feels, Missy, when people don't understand you, but that's the way it is when you're not like everybody else in the whole town. If it's shoes you're lookin' for, I have a pair that would fit your unique personality to a T. They have your special flair written all over them."

Little by little the toughest cynics would fall for his line 'cause there are some things we are all just dying to believe—like when Phil Flam would look the ladies straight in the eye and tell them, "That's the most becoming hair-do ever. I'll bet you came right here straightaway from the beauty parlor." He always came up a winner.

Pretty soon Flam sensed that he was wasting his considerable talent selling shoes. It was abundantly clear that he could sell anybody anything. An idea for his own business struck him when he visited the state fair one lucky day and listened to the hawkers sell their wares. He'd watch them deliver a persuasive spiel as the crowds would begin to gather 'round and every person was hypnotized and just dying to buy something. He was inspired to become a medicine man with a motorized prairie schooner—which looked all the world like a covered wagon from the old West. He concocted a pale amber elixir, made from a good portion of simple syrup, a hint of alcohol, and a nice dose of sarsaparilla. Then he funneled the stuff into eight-ounce (236.59 ml) medicine bottles. The labels on the bottles had a picture of Phil looking as sincere as a body could look and still be human. Calling himself Doc Phil Flam, he hit all the small towns on the circuit and worked the crowds at all the fairs. Oh how the money rolled in!

The golden tones of his resonating voice mesmerized the customers as he chanted the wonders of Flam's health tonic. They loved and adored him as he peddled the powers of his brew:

"Be a better husband,
A more radiant wife
You've never felt
So good in your life."

Flam's tonic cures:
"Coughs, colds,
Sore moles,
Pimples on the belly
And asthma!"

The people believed every word as Phil's litany floated from the make-shift stage. The folks sang his praises and testified to the curative powers of Flam's bottled amber liquid, 'till one sorrowful day when Phil Flam fell ill right smack in front of his own audience. The ten-dollar bills from his sales were still bulging out of his vest and trouser pockets when he was stricken—toppling from the stage and clutching his belly in agony.

"Call a doctor, quick," he groaned.

"No need to call one of them quacks, Phil. Take a swig of your own Flam's Famous Elixir. That'll cure what ails you," his fans assured him.

"I don't want it," he croaked. "Don't you understand. Call a doctor now," Flam implored.

"Don't be a fool, Doc—you've been healing us all this time—now it's your turn to get healed."

"I feel like I'm going to die, for sure," he blubbered, holding his sides.

A sympathetic customer in the crowd actually gave up his own bottle of Phil Flam's Famous Elixir. Others held the Doc down and forcibly poured it into his throat. They soothed and reassured him that it would make him as good as new. He choked and fussed, battling them to no avail. By now he was crying like a babe, "You dumb louts! This stuff won't cure anything! It's about as good as a moonshiner's rot gut."

Everybody stopped—frozen into a tableau of stunned silence. In a hushed whisper a question filled the air, "Did you hear what he said?"

"Sure we heard him. He said he's been selling us worthless rot gut!"

The crowd was angered and humiliated. Finally a vengeful voice shouted out, "Hang the rotten weasel!"

But cooler heads prevailed as another customer said, "Why make trouble for yourself over someone who ain't worth a sack of garbage?" They turned their backs on Phil Flam and left the charlatan to his own ignominious fate, groveling in the dirt.

There's a Sucker Born Every Minute*

For the Teacher

2B Detroit Free Press/Friday, June 1. 1990*

Where are the prizes? 3 charged with scam

by Jocelyne Zablit
Free Press Staff Writer

Hermione Hapless said that when a St. Clair Shores firm told her she was the lucky winner of a 1990 Cadillac, she thought the deal was too good to be true—but also too good to pass up.

A company spokesman told her that for just $599, she could claim her prize, the 67-year-old Waco, Texas, retiree said Thursday.

"I thought it was surely real," Hapless said. "I heard of people winning like that in sweepstakes. But the more I thought about it after I mailed the check the more I became skeptical."

But by then it was too late.

On Thursday, IRS agents and St. Clair Shores police arrested three members of the firm—Lucky Marketing—and charged them with fraud.

Owner Sam Scammer, 42, of St. Clair Shores, manager Dick Connive, 33, of Mt. Clemens and employee Larson E. Goodly, 24, of Warren each face up to five years in prison and $250,000 in fines if convicted.

Their attorney, Dewey Cheatum, declined comment Thursday.

The trio and others allegedly called at least 129 people throughout the country

> **"The more I thought about it after I mailed the check the more I became skeptical."**
> **Hermione Hapless**

with promises of a car, a trip to the Bahamas, a 48-inch television or cash. They were told the company distributes vitamins and they should send money for vitamins and for taxes on the prizes, federal officials said.

IRS spokeswoman Sara Staunch said the firm, which has two offices in St. Clair Shores and one in East Detroit, took in at least $70,000.

Annie May, 79, of Bellflower, Calif, said she was told to send $399 to claim one of four prizes, but the firm settled on $200 since she couldn't afford the larger amount.

"I was foolish," she said Thursday. "I've never done anything like that. It was my mistake."

Hapless said she tries not to get worked up about the matter. "I am angry but I can't afford to have a heart condition and fall to pieces and get sick," she said. "I would have needed that much to go to the hospital."

There's a Sucker Born Every Minute

Point of View—Discussion Questions

1. Why do people believe the promises, the sales pitch or the claims of persons like Phil Flam, who are con artists? What explains the gullibility of the public who fall for such chicanery?

Possible Answer

P.T. Barnum, the showman of circus fame, was purported to have said, "There's a sucker born every minute." But long before that, the ancient Aesop in his famous fables told the story of a shoemaker turned doctor who victimized people and got into the same trouble as Phil Flam. Aesop's story reveals to us that there were gullible people even 2500 years ago.* Among the many reasons people are duped is that they want to believe what they hear; they may be searching for a miracle cure; they may be greedy and eager to make a fast dollar; or they want to improve their appearance. Perhaps there is an innocence in the basic nature of human beings that makes them wish that a remedy for problems is within reach. Perhaps, too, there is the eternal hope that it is possible to get something for almost nothing!

2. In your opinion, what type of person becomes a flimflam artist? If there is talent involved, what kinds of skills does such a person have that makes others trust him or her?

3. Why is it unreasonable when advertisements promise a "get rich quick" offer or want to give you something for nothing? What offers do you know about which should make people suspicious and are found daily on TV, radio or in the print media? Collect some questionable advertisements that sound too good to be true. Bring them to class for analysis. (Remember the warning of the Better Business Bureau which states, "If it sounds too good to be true, it probably is.")

---

*For other cautionary tales to live by, see *Famous Fables for Little Troupers*, by Greta B. Lipson, Ed.D. (Carthage, IL: Good Apple, Inc., 1984.)

There's a Sucker Born Every Minute

Improvisation—Role Play Variations

1. Role-play a scene at the state fair where Phil Flam is making a sales pitch for his elixir to a captive audience. They obviously love him and his cure-all medicine.

2. Invite customers onto the makeshift stage in front of the motorized covered wagon. These eager people will give testimonials on how Phil Flam's Famous Elixir cured them of some disabling illnesses and restored them to health and vigor. They claim their lives were mercifully changed for the better.

3. Enact the last scene where Phil Flam is deathly sick and members of his well-intentioned audience are trying to force him to drink his own phony elixir. As the scene ends, there are varying reactions to the revealed truth that Flam is a phony. Anger moves people in different ways. Some want to go after Phil's hide right there on the spot. A few quieter citizens consider a legal solution to make him pay for his villainy! And then there are those folks who are very embarrassed over their own stupidity.

4. In a group effort, present a "hard-sell" commercial to the class. Select a product or a service among the many you have seen, such as a weight loss program, a dating service or an exterminator. Use props and visual aids. Select the group that had the most outrageous sales pitch.

There's a Sucker Born Every Minute

Writing Suggestions

1. Acting as a consumer affairs group, write an after-school special on con artists, swindlers, and imposters. Warn consumers about how to avoid being exploited by fraudulent or questionable advertisers. Give advice to unsuspecting citizens by describing ploys that are used to prey on the public. Contact your local consumer affairs government agency for additional information.

2. Write a misleading TV, radio or newspaper advertisement for any product or service. Include claims that have no substance in fact. Try to be convincing when presenting these "come-on" lures to the class:

"Lose weight and eat as much as you want." "Grow rich thick hair in a few weeks!" "Be a top executive in thirty days with our dynamic instruction." "Develop into a powerful persuasive speaker after twelve mail order lessons." "Want to knock the girls (or guys) dead with your charm . . . ?" "Earn money like a Wall Street wizard and triple your life savings!"

3. Review advertisements in the print media which make liberal use of propaganda techniques. Copy the exact words and phrases. Try to identify the techniques on the next page.

There's a Sucker Born Every Minute

Writing Suggestions

Glittering Generalities

Shimmer shampoo makes your hair bouncier and alluring.

Plain Folks

Wheat bread like Grandma used to make.

Emotional Appeal

If your love is forever, give her (him) . . . .

Testimonial

The great Butch Kurlansky buys Bruiser Sweat Socks.

Scientific Approach

Four out of five board certified dentists use Dazzler toothpaste.

Snob Appeal

For those in prestigious positions who want to drive in elegance . . .

Band Wagon

Join the savvy, hip kids in your generation and wear cuneiforms.

Transfer

Grouping unrelated things for a stronger effect:

Young and carefree (Is that always true?)

Thick and juicy (Can't it be thick and tough?)

Homegrown and delicious (Can it be homegrown and inferior?)

Name _____

There's a Sucker Born Every Minute

The Gullible Support the Sharpers
Student Comment

Characters: Phil Flam, the flimflam man
              Customers at the state fair

In a paragraph express your feelings about an aspect of this story which you liked or disliked. How would you have changed it?

Alternative: Now that the story has been discussed, explain the proverb above from your point of view.

_____

_____

_____

_____

_____

_____

_____

_____

_____

_____

Chapter 8
The Destiny of David Swan

The Destiny of David Swan

Synopsis

David Swan is a young man who leaves the farm and is on his way to Boston where an uncle has offered him a job in the grocery trade. He walks to the nearest town in the summer heat to wait for the Boston coach. Once there he finds a secluded, mystical little park in which to rest his weary self. Almost as soon as David rolls up his knapsack and puts it under his head, he falls into a deep, delicious slumber. While he sleeps, other characters enter his life fleetingly. Fate stands by teasing his future. A chance at wealth and privilege presents itself, a blissful romance with a lovely woman becomes a possibility, and even Death, a sinister and unexpected guest, waits for David. Through all of these possibilities, the young man sleeps unaware—and finally awakens as he must—to his actual fate.

The Destiny of David Swan

Fate Is a Dark Secret
Concealed from Us All

Retold by Greta B. Lipson

It was harder to say good-bye this morning than he had ever dreamed it could be. But David Swan told himself that he was no longer a child— it was time to leave and make a life for himself elsewhere. There was no future on the farm, he knew it well, but still he was wrenched by the decision and was even a little fearful.

They had all walked out of the house with him—his mother and father, sister and brothers, and of course the dog who faced his loss stoically. And when David turned away to leave, he felt the emotional presence of his family at his back. They were standing—framed by the old house—watching him. He thought that if he allowed himself to look at them one last time their arms would be outstretched as if to call him back in silent remorse at his departure.

*Retold from "David Swan," *The Complete Short Stories of Nathaniel Hawthorne: Seventy-Two Tales of Fantasy and Imagination* (Garden City, New York: Doubleday and Company, Inc., 1959).

The offer of a job from his uncle in Boston came at just the right time. David would be a clerk in the grocery trade, and if he did well and worked hard there would be no telling about the promise of the future. His heart lightened somewhat out of gratitude toward a relative he had never met.

He had set out from the farm at sunrise and was now walking under the blazing noon sun of an August day. The coach wasn't due for at least an hour when he arrived at the center of town. That would be just enough time for David to rest his feet and get relief from the sweltering heat. Surprised and grateful, he found a little grove of trees nestled on a patch of green just off the main street. The leaves arched above like a cool, lacy umbrella as he eased himself onto the soft grass and contemplated the fountain with its offerings of refreshment. No one could have imagined such a secluded retreat in the heart of this bustling intersection.

The bundle of clothes he carried made a soft cushion roll for his head. He stretched out with the intention of enjoying the blue sky filtering through the graceful branches. The cool earth yielded under him. As could be expected he was lulled by the calm of the scene and was swept into a deliciously deep sleep.

Some passersby noticed the young man sleeping soundly. One righteous fellow thought David was in a drunken stupor and included this anecdote in a temperance speech he was to be giving that evening on the evils of drink. Another person saw David and reflected on the pure innocence of his face. Life went on and the farm boy was left alone in his slumber.

Within moments after he had fallen asleep, a fine carriage pulled up at the miniature park and an older, obviously affluent couple stepped out of the carriage. A wheel needed fixing and their servant was preparing to help the coachman with the repairs. The elderly merchant and his wife were returning to Boston and were pleased with this green enclave which offered its gentle shade. Immediately they noticed David and remarked upon the good fortune of the young who could enjoy such relaxed and untroubled sleep—for the weary merchant had the serious problems which beset the very rich.

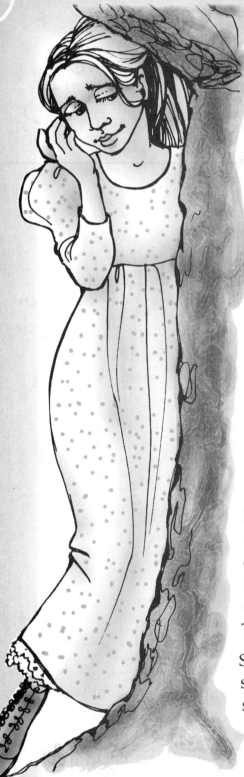

The merchant and his wife carried with them a burden of grief, for they had lost a son, who was their only heir, and there was no one left to whom they could leave their considerable fortune. The wife looked at the slumbering David and perceived a resemblance to their unfortunate, dead son, Henry. She was overcome with emotion, as only a parent could be who had lost a child. She suggested to her husband that they should waken the young lad to discover his true goodness. For he had the appearance of a worthy young man. Perhaps a generous stroke of luck had brought them all together so that this boy could take the place of their own departed Henry.

At that critical moment with ". . . fortune bending over David just ready to let fall a burden of gold," the servant announced that their coach was repaired and ready to travel once again. The old couple were jolted back to reality. They left the park feeling foolish about their effusive impulse toward a young man who was, to them, a total stranger.

No sooner had they departed than a pretty girl walked briskly over the grassy berm into the privacy of the trees. Emily was her name, and she was having a struggle with a broken garter and a falling stocking that had to be rescued out of public view. The park afforded her just the seclusion she needed.

She almost fell over the slumbering David and was so shocked that she blushed, though no one had seen the closeness of the mishap. Emily was overcome with his handsome appearance. "So like a prince," she thought. "He could be my life's companion, and we would make a perfect, loving twosome." She knew he was the right romantic partner for her. It was a strong intuitive sense that filled her with yearning. If only he would open his eyes and instantly discover the same feelings for her.

Emily's father had announced that she was of an age to be married. He was already searching for another person to work in his business, for he was a thriving country merchant. Such a man as David would be considered a candidate for a son-in-law as well. Her father was, as usual, forthcoming about his plans for her. Perhaps it was because she was never consulted in important matters related to her life, that at this very moment, looking at David, she wished desperately that her father's choice could be this noble looking youth whose name was unknown to her.

Though such a radiant future was so close to realization for David, he slept and remained blissfully unconscious of it. What a pity. In a parting gesture Emily brushed her handkerchief against a bee about to settle on David's eyelid, but still he slept without stirring. The shy girl left, bearing her disappointment, as she looked longingly at David one more time.

Sweet Emily walked out of David's life forever, when two suspicious looking men entered the park. They were furtive, dressed in rough attire, with caps pulled down over their eyes looking as if they were about some kind of mischief. And indeed they were. Any chance to turn a dollar would satisfy them, no matter how low the enterprise. They spied David almost immediately and were overjoyed that they had stumbled onto a likely, unconscious victim. No doubt about it, they thought. This was a country bumpkin who probably had an ample roll of cash in the bundle tucked under his head.

Almost with one mind they talked over the quick plan. One of them would search the bundle and the other, who brandished a knife, would hold it to David's heart. If the boy were to awaken while they were about their dirty business, he would be stabbed through the heart swiftly and perhaps they would be richer for the whole incident. They undertook the task with great relish and not a moment's hesitation since they had neither scruples nor decency to deter them. David made things so much easier since he slept like a stone.

All at once there was a tromping sound crashing through the underbrush as a hound of terrifying proportions came shambling out of the green hedges. The lumbering beast sniffed his way into the park, curiously. He eyed the bandits cautiously and then looked at the inert form lying on the ground. This was not a dog to be trifled with. The threat of the animal was an unwelcome turn of events for the two thieves. There was not a moment of indecision when the rascals decided that such a well-groomed monster must have a powerful master who would appear very soon to threaten their thievery. They took off as fast as they could and cursed their rotten luck besides.

All of this had taken place in one single hour. David stirred slowly from his restful sleep to a moderately conscious state—just in time to hear the stagecoach arrive in a clatter of sounds and noises from the passengers. He roused himself hurriedly, brushed his clothes and appeared on the street shouting to the driver. "Hey there. Wait up for another passenger!" He wave furiously to catch the driver's attention.

The Destiny of David Swan

Point of View—Discussion Questions

1. If it is true that our lives are determined by the whims of fate, or destiny or chance, how do we have any influence over the course of events in our lives?

Possible Answer

It would be foolish to deny the role of fate in the scenario of our lives or to deny the inexorable forces of nature or the unremitting effect of social class on all of us. There is so much that is in place for each of us at the time of birth that, some argue, we are almost programmed for our destiny. Others believe that we are the masters of our destiny. Included in this calculation, of course, is the effect of the country in which we live—and our relative freedom, health, education, or personal drive. Even our birth order makes a difference in our lives—if one is the oldest, middle, or youngest in the family. But all things considered—we definitely do make decisions every day of our lives. We do make important choices which have a profound effect upon the quality of our present and our future. To this degree we have some influence upon events and factors which shape our destiny.

2. Consider the decisions that you have the freedom to make on a daily basis. What choices do you make that could have a significant long-term effect on your future? How could a bad decision with regard to the friends you choose be of major importance? Think in terms of school, friends, recreation, and work. Be specific about positive and negative outcomes with regard to your choices.

The Destiny of David Swan
Point of View—Discussion Questions

3. There seem to be some people to whom bad things always happen. A philosopher said, in considering this situation, "Experience without understanding or insight just turns out to be one rotten thing after another." What does that mean to you? Enlarge upon that message. How does your ability to assess information, ask questions, make decisions, and set standards for ethical behavior help you control your life?

4. The great English scientist, Sir Isaac Newton, in his third law of motion states that "For each action there is an equal and opposite reaction." Explain how you think that works in human life.

The Destiny of David Swan
Improvisation–Role Play Variations

1. Assume the role of a research person. Interview a class member who is enacting the part of a teacher, counselor, custodian, or any other interesting adult in the community. Find out what brought them to their career choices and what elements of decision making or fate were factored into their careers.

2. Role-play a scenario in which David awakens while either the old couple, Emily, or the thieves were present. Go beyond the moment in the park and play out the possibilities according to the vision of all the other actors involved in the chance encounter. What happens?

3. Interview David Swan in his home or place of business ten years from the date of his trip to Boston. Ask questions which will reveal to the audience precisely what has taken place in the life of this man who left home to become a clerk in his uncle's business. Does he have any words of advice? Make his life as fascinating, mysterious, or as dull as you wish. In how many directions can a life unfold?

The Destiny of David Swan

Writing Suggestions

1. Taking a thread from the theme of David Swan, weave a story of your own fate if you were born of other parents in a different family or if you lived in Asia, Africa, the Middle East, England, or Eastern Europe. Write a description of this "other" you. How would your life be different? Use your imagination but retain realism. (You could be a beggar on the streets of a Third World nation at the age of four!)

2. Brainstorm a list of famous people. Write a serious or funny biographical sketch where fate intercedes and the life of a famous person takes another direction. What alternative circumstances took them into a different profession or route? (Example: Albert Einstein, one of the greatest scientists of all time: Assume that he did not take a job as a civil servant in a Swiss patent office. Instead—his friendly neighbors, who knew he played the fiddle, offered him a gig in a busy cafe. He accepted the job because he was very poor and needed the extra bucks. The job was so pleasant and satisfying that he didn't finish his doctoral dissertation nor did he pursue any of his research again! What would have happened to $E = MC^2$ and to the world of science?)

3. In Greek mythology the ancients believed that the pattern of a human's life was determined by the Fates, who were the three daughters of Zeus. The sisters were called collectively, the MOIRAI (MOY rye). Each had a special task—Clotho spun the thread of life with light and dark lines which represented sorrow and happiness. Lachesis twisted the thread which made a life strong or weak. And Atropos—the most frightening sister of all—cut the thread which determined the length of a life. The sisters knew the past and everything in the future and no force in the universe could change the course of human events as they designed it.*

---

*Greta B. Lipson, Ed.D., and Sidney M. Bolkosky, Ph.D., *Mighty Myth: A Modern Interpretation of Greek Myths for the Classroom* (Carthage, Illinois: Good Apple, Inc., 1982).

The Destiny of David Swan

Fate Is a Dark Secret Concealed from Us All
Student Comment

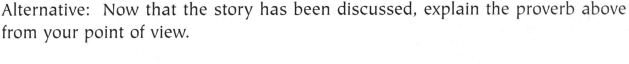

Characters: David Swan   Old couple
             Emily   Robbers

In a paragraph express your feelings about an aspect of this story which you liked or disliked. How would you have changed it?

Alternative: Now that the story has been discussed, explain the proverb above from your point of view.

_____

_____

_____

_____

_____

_____

_____

_____

_____

_____

_____

_____

The Cremation of Sam McGee

The Cremation of Sam McGee*
Synopsis

By Robert W. Service

Sam McGee, from Tennessee, finds himself in the far reaches of the frozen north in the Yukon Territory. He is traveling with his good friend Cap, and together they are mushing their way along the Dawson Trail. On Christmas Day, the brutal cold seems beyond the endurance of Sam who knows he will not survive the rigors of this trip. With thoughts of his balmy Southern home and a fantasy about a final warm resting place, Sam asks Cap to swear that he will cremate Sam's last remains. Through fear and grave physical hardship, Cap tries to fulfill this final obligation to his friend. But no one could believe what finally happens to the corpse of Sam McGee.

The Cremation of Sam McGee

Courage Rises in the Face of Adversity

By Robert W. Service

There are strange things done in the midnight sun
    By the men who toil for gold;
The Arctic trails have their secret tales
    That would make your blood run cold;
The Northern Lights have seen queer sights,
    But the queerest they ever did see
Was that night on the marge of Lake Lebarge
    I cremated Sam McGee.

Now Sam McGee was from Tennessee, where the cotton blooms and blows.
Why he left his home in the South to roam 'round the Pole, God only knows.
He was always cold, but the land of gold seemed to hold him like a spell;
Though he'd often say in his homely way that "he'd sooner live in hell."

On a Christmas Day we were mushing our way over the Dawson Trail.
Talk of your cold! Through the parka's fold it stabbed like a driven nail.
If our eyes we'd close, then the lashes froze till sometimes we couldn't see;
It wasn't much fun, but the only one to whimper was Sam McGee.

And that very night, as we lay packed tight in our robes beneath the snow,
And the dogs were fed, and the stars o'erhead were dancing heel and toe,
He turned to me, and "Cap," says he, "I'll cash in this trip, I guess;
And if I do, I'm asking you that you won't refuse my last request.

Well, he seemed so low that I couldn't say no; then he says with a sort of a
    moan:
"It's the cursed cold, and it's got right hold till I'm chilled clean through to the
    bone.
Yet 'tain't being dead—it's my awful dread of the icy grave that pains;
So I want you to swear that, foul or fair, you'll cremate my last remains."

A pal's last need is a thing to heed, so I swore I would not fail;
And we started on at the streak of dawn but God! he looked ghastly pale.
He crouched on the sleigh, and he raved all day of his home in Tennessee;
And before nightfall a corpse was all that was left of Sam McGee.

There wasn't a breath in that land of death, and I hurried, horror-driven,
With a corpse half hid that I couldn't get rid, because of a promise given;
It was lashed to the sleigh, and it seemed to say: "You may tax your brawn
    and brains,
But you promised true, and its up to you to cremate those last remains."

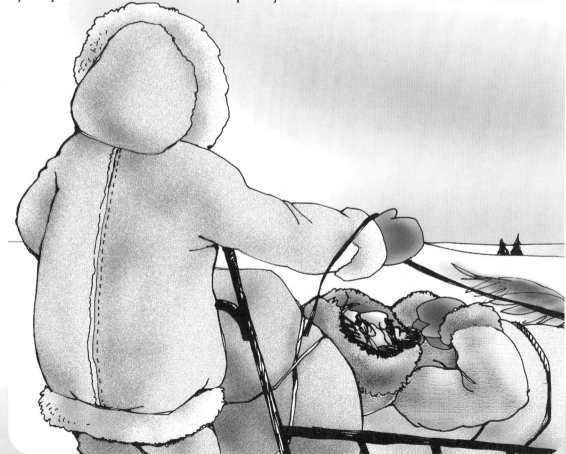

Now a promise made is a debt unpaid, and the trail has its own stern code.
In the days to come, though my lips were dumb, in my heart how I cursed that
    load.
In the long, long night, by the lone firelight, while the huskies, round in a ring,
Howled out their woes to the homeless snows—O God! how I loathed the
    thing.

And every day that quiet clay seemed to heavy and heavier grow;
And on I went, though the dogs were spent and the grub was getting low;
The trail was bad, and I felt half mad, but I swore I would not give in;
And I'd often sing to the hateful thing, and it hearkened with a grin.

Till I came to the marge of Lake Lebarge, and a derelict there lay;
It was jammed in the ice, but I saw in a trice it was called the "Alice May."
And I looked at it, and I thought a bit, and I looked at my frozen chum;
Then "Here," said I, with a sudden cry, "is my cre-ma-tor-eum."

Some planks I tore from the cabin floor, and I lit the boiler fire;
Some coal I found that was lying around, and I heaped the fuel higher;
The flames just soared, and the furnace roared—such a blaze you seldom see;
And I burrowed a hole in the glowing coal, and I stuffed in Sam McGee.

Then I made a hike, for I didn't like to hear him sizzle so;
And the heavens scowled, and the huskies howled, and the wind began to
    blow.
It was icy cold, but the hot sweat rolled down my cheeks, and I don't know
    why;
And the greasy smoke in an inky cloak went streaking down the sky.

I do not know how long in the snow I wrestled with grisly fear;
But the stars came out and they danced about again I ventured near;
I was sick with dread, but I bravely said: "I'll just take a peep inside.
I guess he's cooked, and it's time I looked"; . . . then the door I opened wide.

And there sat Sam, looking cool and calm, in the heart of the furnace roar;
And he wore a smile you could see a mile, and he said: "Please close that door.
It's fine in here but I greatly fear you'll let in the cold and storm—
Since I left Plumtree, down in Tennessee, it's the first time I've been warm.

There are strange things done in the midnight sun
     By the men who toil for gold;
The Arctic trails have their secret tales
     That would make your blood run cold;
The Northern Lights have seen queer sights,
     But the queerest they ever did see
Was that night on the marge of Lake Lebarge
     I cremated Sam McGee.

The Cremation of Sam McGee

Point of View—Discussion Questions

1. Define a hero. Establish criteria for any person, man or woman, whom you would consider to be a heroic character.

   Possible Answer

   In an extraordinary article entitled "Do Teens Hunger for Heroes?" in *Seventeen* magazine, July 1981, the author, Ron Powers, establishes the following standards for a true hero: • "A hero must take risks • A hero must take the risk voluntarily • His or her actions must benefit the world at large • Heroes redeem us." (Redemption is changing one's behavior in response to a positive ideal.)

2. Cap was the name of Sam McGee's friend who, despite his desperate fear, kept his word to Sam. He cremated Sam on the *Alice May*, a derelict barge which was tied up on Lake Lebarge. According to the standards for a hero (which you have established), do you believe that Cap was courageous or heroic? Was he simply driven by fear, a motivation which is less noble? Does he fit the criteria for a hero? Why or why not?

3. We have called many people in popular culture heroes. But now, having defined a hero in more limited terms than in ordinary usage, our standards may have changed. Why does a sports figure, a person in entertainment, a politician, or a prisoner of war *not* qualify as a hero? Keep referring back to Ron Powers' definition as the acid test.

4. Does an act of courage or heroism always imply a physical act? Explain intellectual acts of courage. (Standing up publicly for an ideal or something you believe in, expressing an unpopular opinion, telling the truth—though you may be punished for it—or acts of civil disobedience may all be intellectual acts of courage.)

The Cremation of Sam McGee

Improvisation–Role Play Variations

1. Weary and exhausted after his strange trip home, Cap shares the details of his adventures on the Dawson Trail with his comrades. They ask some very specific questions because they don't believe he was capable of such perseverance in the face of such odds. They especially don't believe the fantasy that Sam McGee expressed his gratitude to Cap from the heart of the fiery crematorium on the barge. Cap responds to the direct questions of his friends and tries vigorously to defend his reputation. Re-create this scene.

2. Cap returns to camp under a cloud. By his own admission he left the body of Sam McGee in the deep snow where there was not even the need to dig a grave. He is criticized harshly by his comrades for not bringing the body back. His defense is that it was senseless to risk his own life just to bring back a dead body. He thinks that such an attitude is illogical. He believes that dragging the body back would have been a meaningless ritual. Some of his friends agree with his logic, others disagree. Assume a point of view for the role play. Generalize two other situations. For example, should a soldier on a field of battle risk his life to rescue the body of a dead comrade in arms? A boy or a girl can assume the role of Cap.

3. Assume the role of a real male or female hero in history. Be prepared to answer questions from the audience about your selfless act. Since self-preservation is the ultimate law of existence, how can it be that you were prepared to sacrifice yourself for the betterment of humankind?

(Prometheus in Greek mythology would be such a hero. He stole fire from the gods to give to humans. He wanted to elevate them from the level of animals and in doing so improve the quality of their lives. The name Prometheus means "forethought," which indicates that he knew fully that he would be punished eternally by the great god Zeus for having committed this act, but this did not deter him.)*

---

*Greta B. Lipson, Ed.D., and Sidney M. Bolkosky, Ph.D., *Mighty Myth: A Modern Interpretation of Greek Myths for the Classroom* (Carthage, Illinois: Good Apple, Inc., 1982).

The Cremation of Sam McGee

Writing Suggestions

1. In the poem, Cap expresses his reactions throughout his ordeal as follows: "It was icy cold but the hot sweat rolled down my cheeks," "I wrestled with grisly fear," "I was sick with dread." From your own experience or what you have heard, what do you think happens to a person physically in an emergency situation which makes it possible for that person to perform with power and speed? Write a description of your own personal reactions in a stressful situation which you have experienced. How does fright sometimes have a reverse reaction which does not produce courage or galvanize action?

2. Recall a heroic act which you have heard or read about currently or in history. Describe the circumstances. From the accounts of the situation, were there any clues about the reasons the hero would risk life and limb to help someone in trouble who may even have been a stranger? Do you believe such courage can be explained logically? Consider intellectual acts of courage as well.

3. Since "The Cremation of Sam McGee" was set in the frozen north, it would be intriguing to research the adventuresome Susan H. Butcher, dog kennel owner and famous "musher" who was, by 1990, a three-time winner of the Iditarod Trail Sled Dog Race in Alaska. The route of the race is from Anchorage to Nome—a formidable, tough 1600 miles of bitter, bone-chilling cold. If you could interview Ms. Butcher, what questions would you be anxious to ask this powerful woman who has met this Herculean challenge? For starters, you may want to know that she was born in Boston, Massachusetts, on December 26, 1954.

Name _____

The Cremation of Sam McGee

Courage Rises in the Face of Adversity
Student Comment

Characters: Sam McGee from Tennessee
              Cap, his friend
              The men at camp

In a paragraph express your feelings about an aspect of this story which you liked or disliked. How would you have changed it?

Alternative: Now that the story has been discussed, explain the proverb above from your point of view.

_____

_____

_____

_____

_____

_____

_____

_____

_____

_____

_____

_____

_____

Chapter 10
A Tail with a Twist

A Tail with a Twist

Synopsis

Mr. MacDonald, a contentious pig farmer, has lived on his Iowa farm, Oinker Acres, for as long as anybody can remember. Mr. Bud Pozey, a porcine land developer, buys the land next door to the farmer and builds Fragrant Meadows, a residential subdivision. In a short time the residents realize that the farm is a serious nuisance, and they want to get rid of the inflexible Mr. MacDonald. But Old Mac refuses to leave his land. The residents are angry, and they take their grievance to the Francis Bacon Community Hall for a civic hearing. They claim that Old MacDonald stands in the way of progress. The outcome is unexpected! (Besides serving the cause of justice— this story has another twist: As you read it through, be a puckish punster and pick out pork parts and piggy allusions amply placed throughout this pugnacious tale. What's your score?)

A Tail with a Twist

Contentious People May Be Pigheaded

By Greta B. Lipson

Mr. MacDonald had owned the farm since he was a young guy. He settled far away from the city and through his desperately hard work Oinker Acres became the most prosperous pig farm in Iowa. As we all know, life changes and many years later the city grew toward the farm. That's when property developers bought the farm next door to Mac. They built houses in the meadow, put the babbling brook into a sewer, and then named the subdivision Fragrant Meadows.

Now something you have to know about Mac was that he had been a mean-spirited old coot even when he was young! Nobody ever got too familiar with him. Even his friends called him Mister. As his wife, Trichina, pointed out, he wasn't much for social amenities, but you couldn't make a silk purse out of a sow's ear. Besides, she said affectionately, he had other good qualities.

On any morning, at Shoat's Cafe, over sausage and eggs, you could hear the ex-farmers gossiping about Old MacDonald and his pigheaded resistance to prosperity in the community. His former neighbors had all given up their farms, sold out to the developers, and joined the so-called wave of progress. But not Mac.

After the first families moved into Fragrant Meadows, things settled down for a while. Life was as smooth as a piglet's snout until the developers went hog-wild again. Bud Pozey, the builder, tried his level best to persuade Mac to sell his land. The "big boys" wanted that farm in the worst way. It seems the families in the subdivision were complaining that Old MacDonald was an intolerable nuisance.

When the developers offered to cut a deal with Mac, he said to Trichina, "No sir! I'm not selling to those spoilers. Not in a pig's eye!" He was a stubborn rascal. Trichina and Mac knew they were lucky to get such fat offers for the farm. Besides that—Bud Pozey had even offered Mac a cushy-sounding job. But the old farmer didn't trust any of them. "Sounds like a pig in a poke to me!" he said. "Those guys are as slippery as a spoon in a lard bucket."

The fact is that Mac loved his life as a farmer and though it demanded sacrifice and hardship, he cared deeply about the land. Both he and his wife had come from farming families, and it was all they had ever known. Besides that (and this may sound funny to you) Mac had an enduring affection for the porkers he raised. Trichina and Mac were determined to stay.

Maybe matters were resolved on the pig farm but the misery of the hapless residents at Fragrant Meadows increased daily. "No friendly barbecue parties for us anymore," Mr. Fretful announced. "That last experience was the pits, with all those barnyard smells floating in a cloud over the food on the picnic table. What a way to gag our dinner guests." To make matters worse, their kid, little Franny Fretful had a stuffed nose that was running nonstop from the pesticides in the air.

In another household Mrs. Barrow complained to her husband over the breakfast table. "How could that porcine builder, Bud Pozey, do this to us? What about zoning laws?" She had been listening to the roaring of MacDonald's tractor since sunrise.

Her husband was exasperated. "It's like I told you before—we're all properly zoned—Old MacDonald is zoned for his farm and we're zoned for our subdivision. Don't you get it? We're all legal, but the trouble is we're living side-by-side. Old Mac's not going to give up his farm, and we can't sell our house to anybody."

"It's time for a showdown," the residents decided. "We can't live next door to the stink, the chemicals, and the disgusting animal sounds, but Mac insists upon his property rights, too."

Inevitably the neighbors took their grievance to the Francis Bacon Community Hall for a civic hearing. The place was jammed with people. Inside they were talking their heads off and outside it was crowded with protesters carrying placards. Some of the signs read: "Farmers have rights too."—"Oinker Acres is a public nuisance."—"Some slops don't care how they live."—"A pigsty is an eyesore."

After a long, heated meeting, the decision was announced by Hamilton Hocks who, though he was known to be a deadly bore, was always respected for his integrity. In a majority resolution, it was concluded that Old MacDonald's farm could stay just where it was and that was the final word.

Before the meeting was dismissed, some angry folks stood up and shouted, "I don't believe this!"—"You call this justice? I call it hogwash!" "We demand an explanation!"

Old Hamilton Hocks rose from his seat and cleared his throat. There was a hush. "Old Mac has been on that farm for 25 years. Sure it's hog heaven and you don't like it. But remember. You folks made a choice and moved next door to a working farm of your own free will. Mac didn't move next door to you!"

The case is now in litigation in the courts in Suidae, Iowa. The complainants were not going to be hog-tied by a decision made at a civic hearing. This is a true story. Only the names have been changed to protect the innocent.

A Tail with a Twist

For the Teacher

In the writing of educational books, it has been the author's practice to enlist the expertise of skillful people and, most especially, interested teachers who are willing to critique the material. The most fascinating result of all of this is discovering what others see in the material and how they would use it. Even more interesting, is the strong response a topic evokes! These responses are always a wonderful revelation to the author. The following incisive critique and social commentary by Lorene Sterner demonstrates this point, relative to "A Tail with a Twist." Her letter makes a strong case for teachers to use materials from whichever perspective they consider to be most effective!

A Tail with a Twist

For the Teacher

May 31, 1990

Dear Greta,

I read the story and my opinion is that it is a good story. Good meaty issues (hardy har har). As someone who feels strongly about farms-turning-agribusiness, I would really love to see this story included, if only to get a little consciousness-raising out and about as to what is behind that styro-tray of pork chops you get in the supermarket.

The problem? You have embellished to the point where the story becomes a vocabulary-building exercise. It's amusing, but loses its "twist." I get no sense that MacDonald is, in fact, a character from real life (affection for pigs notwithstanding). I think you could make the point that many farmers have grown up on farms, know of no other life-style, and have worked extraordinarily hard to maintain their farms—gigantic loans, piles of paperwork to comply with federal rules for subsidies, plus the simple fact that farming is extremely dangerous. (I could tell you terrible stories of farm accidents that maim and kill but Bill could, too.) After a lifetime of devoting efforts to producing cheap, healthy food for the public, there should be some irony in being reviled as a public nuisance. As the bumper sticker says, "Farming is everybody's bread and butter."

And there is the fact that the need for affordable housing is tremendous. It's not luxury condos that are being built in these areas; rich people go where there are scenic views, room for their stables and tennis courts, and privacy. Farmlands tend to be developed into moderately priced (ha!) lots for families anxious to flee the crime and deterioration of the city. These are not people who can afford to litigate endlessly to stop what they perceive is a nuisance and a danger; we're talking a scenario more like Love Canal. There is more to the juxtaposition of farm and residential, though, than noise and offensive smells when the wind is right.

You can bet in a real-life situation there would be lawsuits against MacDonald for farm-related respiratory disorders (my father gets instantaneous pneumonia whenever he enters a hog barn); organic waste contaminating groundwater; pesticide/herbicide spray drifting into the subdivision and leading to more respiratory problems, central nervous system disorders and cancer. There would probably be a left-wing protest against inhumane penning and treatment of food animals, too, with charges that MacDonald uses antibiotics and hormones to boost weight gain.

What about zoning? You bring up the Z word, but the bottom line is the same for any part of the law—the rules are fair only if the people who formulate them are fair and forward thinking. Where was the zoning board when this development was put up? Buying big cars with their kick-back checks? Where was MacDonald, by the way? You can bet that he wouldn't be happy to hear the housing was going in next to his alfalfa—no farmer in his right mind wants suburban kids on ATV's tearing up the winter wheat, and letting their untrained dogs run loose on his land to attack livestock.

(Study question: What is the long-term cost to society when high-quality farmland is developed for housing, and less fertile land is used for raising food—which requires use of more fertilizers, pesticides and herbicides?)

I know this is a diatribe rather than a critique, but these are issues which are currently being fought out piecemeal in the courts when, in fact, there is urgent need for broad-based policies to be formulated in order to preserve the public interest. This in itself causes me some serious concern. We either dictate to our population and their development, or they dictate to us. So where are our famous rights to Life, Liberty, and The Pursuit of Happiness? Are these rights only a function of ample resources like land? You can see why I like this story. It can be argued from many different positions, and you can drag in everything but the kitchen sink. (From the audience: "Yeh, what about the kitchen sink? You got anything against plumbing?" Threats of union reprisal offstage . . .) So I will ask please, please, if you can bear the thought, go back, tighten it up, focus on MacDonald as a hardworking agri-operator and Marlene Jones as the single mother of four who is worried about her son's asthma getting worse since they moved near the farm. Let the kids play with the pig theme. Building dramas about the "Swinal Solution" and "Neither a lender nor a farrower be" are fun, but you have more important things to talk about.

Your sincere and loquacious critic,
Lorene Sterner

---

*Reprinted with permission of Lorene Sterner, 1990, Ann Arbor, Michigan.

A Tail with a Twist

Point of View—Discussion Questions

NOISE POLLUTION health hazard?

HE WAS HERE FIRST

1. After the homes were bought in Fragrant Meadows and the families moved in, they complained that Farmer MacDonald was creating a serious nuisance. The worst part was the health hazard. He sprayed chemicals on his crops which were carried by the wind to the new houses. He often plowed his fields with a noisy tractor early in the morning and woke up the entire population. Besides all that, his animals stank. In the face of such strong evidence, how could the Civic Executive Committee decide in favor of Old Mac's right to stay?

Possible Answer

The legal concept of "coming to the nuisance" is illustrated by this story and that is what made the difference in the decision. Old MacDonald was there first! The pig farm had been established far from the city for many years. Eventually the city spread out and finally came to the nuisance! It was the builders, after all, who made the independent business decision to develop the subdivision right next door to Oinker Acres.*

2. In what ways could the local environmentalists be unhappy with the threat to the environment created by all the people involved: the farmer, the developers, and the home owners?

---

*Greta B. Lipson, Ed.D., and Eric B. Lipson, J.D., *Everyday Law for Young Citizens* (Carthage, Illinois: Teaching & Learning Company, 2000).

A Tail with a Twist

Point of View—Discussion Questions

3. MacDonald, the pig farmer, was criticized by his farmer friends for refusing to go forward with change and "progress." It was their assumption that if the community experienced change and expansion, it automatically meant benefits for everyone. But does change always mean something better? In what ways can technological progress create serious social problems?

   - Change can cause unemployment as people are replaced by machines.
   - Change can also create more employment with greater demands on industrial energy which in turn creates more pollution and industrial wastes.
   - These factors, above, affect the food we eat and the air we breathe.
   - Technology in its march forward may bring the destruction of natural resources.
   - The incursion of new construction can be a threat to the survival of wildlife and the delicate balance of the food chain.
   - As a community grows, the costs of institutions and services increase. This creates a greater need for tax support, which in turn requires more business and industry.

A Tail with a Twist

Improvisation—Role Play Variations

1. Role-play the Civic Executive meeting with all parties represented: farmer MacDonald and his wife Trichina; the residents of Fragrant Meadows; the land developers; and the residents of the city of Suidae, Iowa. Each group is there out of self-interest. Select a person to chair the meeting who can control the group, mediate trouble, and ensure a fair hearing for all.

2. Enact a different citizens' meeting. One group of good citizens are unemployed. They are in support of the Bud Pozey Land Developers coming into town, putting up a big shopping mall, and building homes, schools, and roads. They are opposed to a city building code which would limit and prohibit these sweeping plans for construction. They believe that the most important issue is employment which would be guaranteed by Pozey's ambitious plans. A different group of good citizens are in favor of a restrictive building code. They are very worried about the destructive effects of major construction on their community. They ask the question: How can we resolve the problem of unemployment and still protect the beauty and integrity of the town and its woods and lakes?

3. On Earth Day, April 22, you and a group of friends organize a committee to heighten the awareness of the community to the dangers of pollution. The name of the new organization is Protect the Interests of Good Environment, for which the acronym is P.I.G.E. (pronounced piggy). Your group is mainly concerned about the big imposing smokestacks of the local electric power company which belch smoke and spread pollutants, causing acid rain. Your committee has the inspired idea to have a big mega- watt rock concert to protest the dangerous smoke and enlist the support of the people. The local electric power company sends a spokesperson to talk to you about your slamming his company. He points out to you that the energy needed to give electric power to the rock group for their musical extravaganza will be produced in his coal-fired plant. What does each side of this dilemma (the committee and the electric company representatives) have to say to each other?

A Tail with a Twist
Writing Suggestions

1. We live in a free society where the law functions to balance the rights of property owners who have different interests from each other. Concerning the limits to freedom, there is an expression in the law that says: "One person's rights extend only as far as the other person's nose." How would you explain that quote in a short paragraph?

2. After discussing "A Tail with a Twist," you have heard arguments for and against progress: the advantages of more jobs due to change, the effect of change on the environment, and the quality of life in the present and the future. If you had to identify your strongest bias relative to these issues, what would it be? Begin your paper with the header: "I feel most strongly about the importance of . . . (employment, environment, balance, etc.).

3. Just for the fun of it, read through the story "A Tail with a Twist" and make a list of all the words which suggest or remind you of pigs! Watch for some scientific or technical words as well. If you encounter fancy-sounding names or strange words, you may need a dictionary or an encyclopedia. Of course, people who live in Iowa may not have any trouble at all. Why is that true?

Words from the Story That Suggest Pigs

tail; pigheaded; oinker, fragrant; shoats; sausage; Trichina; Barrow; sow's ear; piglet's snout; porcine; porker; barbecue; Francis Bacon; slops; sty; Hamilton Hocks; bore; hogwash; Suidae, Iowa (a fictitious place); hog-tied; lard . . . .

4. Add your own sentence or paragraph to any part of the story in which you include references to pigs. It must make sense in the context of the story. For example:

   - The families picnicked at Porker's Park on Loin Lagoon.
   - Professor Avoirdupois did research on hogs
   - Everyone in town shopped at the Pig Wiggle Food Mart.
   - They liked to pig out on barbecued ribs.

A Tail with a Twist

Contentious People May Be Pigheaded
Student Comment

Characters: Mr. MacDonald, a pig farmer   Mr. Hamilton Hocks
               Trichina, his wife   Farmers
               Residents of Fragrant Meadows   Citizens of Suidae, Iowa

In a paragraph express your feelings about an aspect of this story which you liked or disliked. How would you have changed it?

Alternative: Now that the story has been discussed, explain the proverb above from your point of view.

_____

_____

_____

_____

_____

_____

_____

_____

_____

_____

_____

_____

Bibliography

Author unknown. "Sand Art, on Deadline," *The New York Times*, August 13, 1989, Section 22E.

Goldstein, Eleanor C., editor. *Social Issues Resources Series*, Inc., Boca Raton, Florida, P.O. Box 2507.

Hawthorne, Nathaniel. "David Swan.". *The Complete Short Stories of Nathaniel Hawthorne: Seventy-Two Talks of Fantasy and Imagination*. Garden City, New York: Doubleday and Company, Inc., 1959.

Lipson, Greta B., and Eric B. Lipson. *Everyday Law for Young Citizens*. Carthage, Illinois: Teaching & Learning Company, 2000.

Lipson, Greta B. *Famous Fables for Little Troupers*. Carthage, Illinois, Good Apple, Inc., 1984.

Lipson, Greta B. *Fast Ideas for Busy Teachers*. Carthage, Illinois: Good Apple, Inc., 1989, p. 13.

Lipson, Greta B., and Sidney M. Bolkosky. *Mighty Myth: A Modern Interpretation of Greek Myths for the Classroom*. Carthage, Illinois, Good Apple, Inc., 1982.

Montague, Ashley, and Edward Darling. *The Ignorance of Certainty*. New York: Harper & Row, 1970.

Powers, Ron. *"Do Teens Hunger for Heroes?" Seventeen*, July 1981, p. 108.

Service, Robert W. *"The Cremation of Sam McGee," Collected Poems of Robert Service*. New York: Dodd, Mead & Co., 1940.

Vitz, Paul C. "The Use of Stories in Moral Development," *American Psychologist*. Vol. 45, No. 6., Washington, D.C.: American Psychological Association, Inc., June 1990, pp. 709-720.

Yolen, Jane, editor. *Favorite Folktales from Around the World*. New York: Random House, 1986.

Notes